MEMOIR
of
CATHARINE BROWN
A
Christian Indian
of the
Cherokee Nation

By Rufus Anderson, A. M.
Assistant Secretary of the American Board of Commissioners of Foreign Missions

AND

THE
LITTLE
OSAGE CAPTIVE,
AN
Authentic Narrative.

BY ELIAS CORNELIUS.

COMPILED & TRANSCRIBED BY
JEFF BOWEN

NATIVE STUDY
Gallipolis, Ohio
USA

Copyright © 2025
by Jeff Bowen

Memoir of Catharine Brown A Christian Indian of the Cherokee Nation

Original publishing: 1825
Publisher: Boston: Samuel T. Armstrong, and Crocker and Brewster;
New York: John P. Haven
1825

The Little Osage Captive An Authentic Narrative

Original publishing: 1822
Publisher: Boston: Samuel T. Armstrong, and Crocker and Brewster;
New York: John P. Haven
1822

Published by:

Native Study LLC
Gallipolis, OH
www.nativestudy.com

2025

Library of Congress Control Number: 2025910405

ISBN: 978-1-64968-180-5

Made in the United States of America.

This transcription is

Dedicated to

the sacrifice of those from Brainerd Mission

and

In Memory of

John Alan Jessing (1966-2025),

a good heart and a good soul, who loved the Cherokee.

Table of Contents

Introduction	vii
Memoir of Catharine Brown (1825)	1
The Little Osage Captive (1822)	103
Index (Combined)	169

INTRODUCTION

Catharine Brown's life became an example of the purest form of intercession between a human and God for another. Selfless! Like Paul achieving the third level of heaven, seeking to be where God resides while he still lived among human beings. Her heart was in His hands and she gave it willingly, with the purest faith as a child. Referenced from: *(First Nations Version, An INDIGENOUS TRANSLATION of the NEW TESTAMENT 2021.)* 2 Corinthians 12:1-7:

SACRED VISIONS AND SPIRITUAL EXPERIENCES
"¹It does not seem like a good thing for me to keep 'bragging like this,' but I now want to tell you about the sacred visions shown to me by the Great Spirit.

"²⁻³Let me tell you the story of a man I know, a follower of the Chosen One. Fourteen winters ago this man was taken up into the highest place in the spirit-world above.[a] If this happened to him in the body or outside the body, I do not know. Only the Great Spirit knows. ⁴This man was taken up into Creator's Beautiful Garden,[b] where he heard mysterious words that human beings are not permitted to speak.

"⁵I will brag about that man, but as for myself I will boast only in how small and weak I am. ⁶It would not be a foolish thing for me to brag about this, because I would be speaking the truth about myself. But I will hold back from saying too much, so that none of you will think too highly of me beyond what you hear me say and see me do.

"⁷The things that were shown to me were so mysterious and powerful that I was given a thorn to stab me where I was weak, a messenger from Accuser (Satan) to prick my pride and keep me humble."

---

[a] Often translated in other English translations as "the third heaven"
[b] Lit. *paradise*

I had a friend on the Cherokee Reservation in North Carolina who I use to say that when she prayed God listened. It wasn't because she thought she was special it was because she loved Him so much and He knew it.... Now she is with Him having reached that third level being in His actual presence. God Bless You Joyce.

Catharine Brown went to the Brainerd Mission during the early 1800's. She felt it was hallowed ground. She accepted Christ there. During the 1990's I went to that hallowed ground. Finding the cemetery secured and too long ago to remember who unlocked that gate at the time allowing me entrance. What I found then was a small mission cemetery surrounded by a chain linked fence covered with vegetation. Hardly a soul had any idea it sat along the edge of this huge bustling mall parking lot with hundreds of cars parked all around and a strip mall on its other side. Just next to its gate sat an old blond brick structure of what used to be a small Sears outlet. Since visiting during that time it has been found out that the DAR and a few local organizations have preserved the cemetery nicely. I went in and didn't wonder much among the markers, there seemed very few, likely most disintegrated through many winters. The gray sandstone markers except for maybe the Rev. Mr. Worchester's and a few more could be read and many more were nondescript and faded (many marked with stones and likely less than one hundred graves) but the astounding thing was the thought of so many Cherokee either coming by horse or a foot had crossed that ground and left with such commitment to God. While many may have felt the Mission a failure those that left in His grace didn't think so. While the few people beneath these stones, though empty vessels, had stayed and were with me there at that moment.

I've read a few articles where a few historians stated that the Mission for the most part was a failure and met with resistance. Well, naturally there likely was some resistance from both red and white. It was hard times. The Indians were being pushed out. Many Cherokees had gone out West to avoid being persecuted by a white surge. There were treaties being drawn up for what was called the Reservees during that time period of 1817 and 1819, that if the Cherokee gave allegiance to the United States they could be given a section of land (640 acres) to settle on rather than being eventually removed. Which fully happened during the Trail of Tears, 1838-39.

The main thing that needs to be stressed is that I don't think there was failure in this Mission or any others that they built. If you read these two volumes the people involved, at the time, never felt that these entities failed in any form. They felt that they were of the greatest success and never failed to reach out well beyond their bounds not just to other people but their own families entirely. They knew God was reinforcing their every effort through the missions they were creating. They understood the power behind each encounter because it wasn't them. The very Spirit in their lives guided the development of every mission, through the Lord, to those involved, failure wasn't an option.

Catharine Brown didn't want to leave that holy ground but God had other plans for her. Though she was on this earth a short time it was just the right amount of time for Him and she was pleased.

She feared she didn't give Him enough time, she had thoughts of losing Him by not thinking of Him enough. In thinking about it and the humbleness of her heart she must have thought she didn't deserve His gift as none ever do, especially since on a human level it is so much to comprehend that He stays within us faithfully day in and day out. To be so in love with the only true God is a wonderful thing. We at times fail in realizing how much He truly did sacrifice. He didn't go through excruciating sorrow and pain for a few He went through it for all of mankind throughout the ages. Unless you personally ask Him into your heart and feel the joy of Him occupying your every fiber you won't or can't understand.

There is nothing like it, ever, and He has opened that door all you have to do is walk through it. He knows your failures now and in the future and even before you were born. But no matter what, once you have allowed His Spirit in, you are no longer an empty vessel. Satan may harass you, but he'll never own you. God doesn't give you up, ever!....

While reading a book about the Civil War, not quoting the exact words but the story went something like this: A couple spies were caught, an officer was going to let one go and execute the other. In panic one soldier said, "I am not a Christian and I have three children and I am afraid to die." The other said, "I am a Christian and I don't have a family but I am not afraid to die." The second man was spared. These lines were quoted for emphasis. (Figure it out.)

Catharine Brown overcame death because she didn't know death, she knew life because she took up that (new) mantle of life through Christ. Catharine Brown prayed for others and it seemed like when she prayed for herself it was to be with those who felt like she did about her Savior Jesus Christ. In her life He was the Alpha and Omega.

Also while reading this volume you will find added Elias Cornelius's, *The Little Osage Captive*, who ended up within the ranks of Brainerd's marvelous existence also; another heart rendering story. This little book speaks out today as it did then over 200 years ago. Enjoy!

Jeff Bowen
Gallipolis, OH
NativeStudy.com

*Please remember any misspellings or incorrect grammar found within these two manuscripts has been transcribed from original record 200 years ago and the style of that time.

"Then raising herself in the bed & wiping a tear, that was falling from her eye.— She with a sweet smile began to relate what God had done for her soul, while upon that sick bed." Page 142.

Boston, Sam.l T. Armstrong and Crocker & Brewster. New York: John P. Haven.

MEMOIR

of

CATHARINE BROWN

A

Christian Indian

of the

Cherokee Nation

By Rufus Anderson, A. M.
*Assistant Secretary of the American Board of
Commissioners of Foreign Missions*

BOSTON:
SAMUEL T. ARMSTRONG, AND CROCKER AND BREWSTER.
NEW YORK: JOHN P. HAVEN.
1825.

DISTRICT OF MASSACHUSETTS, to wit:
District Clerk's Office.

BE IT REMEMBERED, that on the twentieth day of December, A.D. 1824, in the forty-ninth year of the Independence of the United States of America, *Samuel T. Armstrong,* of the said District, has deposited in this office the title of a book, the right whereof he claims as Proprietor, in the words following, *to wit:*

"Memoir of Catharine Brown, a Christian Indian of the Cherokee nation. By Rufus Anderson, A. M. Assistant Secretary of the American Board of Commissioners for Foreign Missions."

In Conformity to the Act of the Congress of the United States, intitled, "An act for the encouragement of learning, by securing the copies of maps, charts and books, to the authors and proprietors of such copies, during the times therein mentioned;" and also to an act, intitled, "An act supplementary to an act, intitled, An act for the encouragement of learning, by securing the copies of maps, charts and books, to the authors and proprietors of such copies during the times therein mentioned; and extending the benefits thereof to the arts of designing, engraving and etching historical, and other prints."

JNO. W. DAVIS,
Clerk of the District of Massachusetts.

PREFACE.

THIS Memoir was commenced as a biographical article for the Missionary Herald. In its progress, however, the materials were found to be so abundant, as to suggest the inquiry whether a distinct publication were not expedient.

Such a publication being advised, by the Prudential Committee of the Board of Missions, it is now respectfully offered to those who feel interested in the success of missionary efforts.

The author is not conscious of having exaggerated a single fact, nor of having made a single statement not drawn from authentic documents. His object has been to give a plain and true exhibition of the life and character of a very interesting convert from heathenism.

The hope is cherished, that this little volume will augment the courage, animate the zeal, and invigorate the efforts, of the friends of missions, in their benevolent attempts to send the Gospel of Jesus Christ to all nations.

Missionary Rooms,
 Boston, Mass. Dec. 1824.

CONTENTS.

CHAPTER I.

HER HISTORY UNTIL SHE ENTERED THE MISSION SCHOOL AT BRAINERD.

Her nativity.—Notice of her parents.—Ignorance of her people.—Her triumph over temptation.—A missionary station commenced at Chickamaugah, and named Brainerd.—She becomes a member of the school,- -   9

CHAPTER II.

FROM HER ENTERING THE SCHOOL AT BRAINERD, UNTIL HER REMOVAL BY HER PARENTS.

Her appearance when she entered the school.—Her diligence and progress.—Her religious knowledge.—Character of her teachers.—Her conversion, and solicitude for her people.—Instance of earnest prayer.—Prospect of her removal.—Her baptism.—Temporary absence.—Admission to the church.—The early success at Brainerd uncommon.—The chief obstacles to success among the Indians.—Visit of the

CONTENTS.

Treasurer of the American Board.—His account of the school, and description of Catharine.—She is removed from Brainerd.—Is visited by one of the missionaries.—Letters from her to her friends,- - - 14

CHAPTER III.

FROM HER RETURN TO BRAINERD, UNTIL SHE TAKES CHARGE OF A SCHOOL AT CREEK-PATH.

Benefits resulting from her being taken from the school.—Her return.—Letters.—Her brother David a member of the school.—His conversion.—Catharine and David visit their sick father.—A school established near Mr. Brown's.—Account of John Arch.—Efforts of Catharine and David at Brainerd,—The latter goes to New-England,—His subsequent history.—A female teacher wanted at Creek-Path.—Catharine undertakes this service.—Letters,- - - - - - - - - - - - - - - - - - - 30

CHAPTER IV.

FROM HER TAKING CHARGE OF A SCHOOL AT CREEK-PATH, UNTIL HER SICKNESS.

Extracts from her diary.—Her school.—Conversion of her parents, and others of the family.—She and her family visit Brainerd.—Letter from the chiefs at Creek-Path.—Traits in Catharine's character.—Further extracts from her diary.—Eulogium of her brother John.—She visits Huntsville.—Estimation in which she was there held.—Goes to reside with her parents.—Apprehensions respecting her health.—Goes to Brainerd for medical aid.—Returns.—Letters to different friends,- - - -   45

CHAPTER V.

HER SICKNESS AND DEATH.

Brief agitations of her mind.—Her love for her people.—Is visited by Dr. Campbell.—Letter to Mrs. Campbell.—Alarming symptom in her disease.—Her resignation and consolations.—Dr. Campbell advises her removal to Limestone.—State of her mind at this time.—Strong manifestations of affection for her at Creek-Path.—Account of her removal.—Temporary improvement in her health.—Dictates a letter to her brother David.—Hopes of her recovery relinquished.—This fact stated to her father and herself.—Her last hours, death, and burial.—Monument over her grave,- - - - - - - - - -   72

CHAPTER VI.

HER CHARACTER.

Her mental characteristics.—Her attainments in intellectual and moral science.—Changes in her affections.—Her Christian conduct.—CONCLUSION.—The excellencies in

CONTENTS.

her character a result of missionary labour.—How much can be made of the Indian character.—Grounds of encouragement.—Importance of present efforts.—Civilization never precedes Christianity.—The life of Catharine an appeal to the community.- - - - - -   85

MEMOIR

of

CATHARINE BROWN.

CHAPTER I.

HER HISTORY UNTIL SHE ENTERED THE MISSION SCHOOL AT BRAINERD.

Her nativity.—Notice of her parents.—Ignorance of her people.—Her triumph over temptation.—A missionary station commenced at Chickamaugah, and named Brainerd.—She becomes a member of the school.

CATHARINE BROWN was born about the year 1800. The place of her nativity was a beautiful plain, covered with tall forest trees, in a part of the country belonging to the Cherokee Indians, which is now called Wills-Valley, and is within the chartered limits of the State of Alabama. It is between the Raccoon and Lookout mountains, twenty-five miles south-east of the Tennessee river. David, the brother of Catharine, says, that the name, by which the place is known among his countrymen, is *Tsu-sau-ya-sah*, or *the ruins of a great city*. But, if such ruins ever existed, all traces of them have long since disappeared.

The Indian name of Catharine's father, is *Yau-nu-gung-yah-ski*, which signifies *the drowned by a bear*. He is, however, known among the whites by the name of *John Brown*. The Cherokee name of her mother is *Tsa-luh*. The whites call her *Sarah*.—Neither of Catharine's parents understand the English language. They are now about sixty years of age. Since the

MEMOIR OF

decease of the daughter, whose history and character are to form the subject of this memoir, they have removed beyond the Mississippi river, to the Arkansas Territory, whither a part of the Cherokee nation of Indians have emigrated, within the last fifteen or twenty years.[1]

Mr. Brown is represented as possessing a mind more than commonly discerning; yet as having, when the missionaries first

---

[1] A more particular account of the family of Catharine, may be acceptable to the reader.

Mr. John Brown was the son of a man named Brown, who has long been dead. It is not known whether he was a white man, or partly Indian. The mother of Mr. Brown was a "full-blooded" Cherokee. So, also, was the mother of Mrs. Brown; but her father was white. Catharine's parents were brought up like others of their nation;—no better acquainted with the language, religion, manners, or customs of the white people.

Mr. Brown has had three wives. The first had two children, neither of whom are living. One of these children became a man of much distinction. In the Creek war he had the title of Colonel, as he commanded a large number of Cherokees, who made a part of the army under General Jackson. He was severely wounded at the battle of the *Horse-shoe*; but recovered, and died subsequently of a fever, or consumption. He is said to have possessed uncommon powers of mind, and to have exerted much influence among his people. He is familiarly referred to by the name of *Col. Dick Brown.*

The children of Sarah, the second and present wife of Mr. Brown, were *John*, who died in the Christian faith, February 1822, leaving a widow, *Susannah*, who is a professor of religion; *Catharine*, the subject of this memoir; and *David*, of whose piety hopes have been entertained for almost five years.

The children of the third wife, named *Wottee*, or *Betsey*, who, for some years, has been living in the Arkansas Territory, are *Polly*, (or Mrs. Gilbreth,) *Alexander*, *Susan*, and *Edmund*. Polly and Susan are esteemed pious.

Sarah and Betsey lived with Mr. Brown at the same time. But some difficulty arising, the latter separated from him.

Sarah was the wife of a man named Webber, before she married Mr. Brown. The children, by this marriage, are *Betsey*, (now Mrs. Looney,) a professor of religion, and *Walter*, called Col. *Webber*. He was at Washington city, about two years since, and possesses a handsome property. These children were quite young, when their father died. Col. Webber is now about thirty-five years old.

It appears, therefore, that of Mr. Brown's family no less than *nine* have become hopefully pious, within the last seven years, viz. Mr. and Mrs. Brown, John, Catharine, David, Polly, Susan, Susannah, and Mrs. Looney.

The reader will be apt to infer, when he sees individuals called by names and titles, with which he is familiar, that they are very much like other individuals, whom he has known under similar titles; in short, that they are civilized and intelligent persons. Such an inference, however, is not warranted. The mere possession of an English name, in an Indian country, is no evidence that the person thus distinguished is able to speak the English language; much less, that his habits are those of civilized life, or that his mind has been in any degree cultivated.

As to the military titles of captain, major, colonel, and even general, they are conferred as a matter of courtesy, in consequence of some sort of undefined authority, which is exercised over others, and which is supposed to bear some distant analogy to the authority, implied in these titles, among us. Of course, the titles are conferred by the whites. In some instances, when Indian auxiliaries have been employed in active warfare, by European governments, or by the United States, individuals may have received regular commissions. Mr. Brown and his son John, were both denominated Captain.

saw him, but few ideas on the subject of religion. He believed in a Supreme Being, the author of the visible creation, and that there is state of rewards and punishments, after the present life; and appeared conscious, that there were things implied in this short creed, of which he had no distinct apprehension; such as the character of the Supreme Being, the nature of the rewards and punishments, and the manner in which the one is to be obtained, and the other avoided. He seemed to have no notion of forgiveness of sin upon any terms. When told of these things, he said he had never heard of them before.

Concerning the *mother*, less is known to the writer of this memoir. Her religious knowledge, if equal to that of her husband, did not probably exceed it. She is represented as having been more attentive to neatness and good order, in the internal arrangements of the family, and more conversant with the duties of domestic life, than her countrywomen generally.

Ignorant as were the parents of Catharine, on the most important subjects, they were among the more intelligent class of their people. Till within a few years, the Cherokees had scarcely begun to feel an impulse towards civilization. Indeed, as a nation, they were almost entirely destitute of the means of intellectual, or moral culture. In a very few instances, a youth was sent to school in the white settlements, bordering on the Indian territory; and still more rarely, perhaps, an outcast from civilized society would undertake for a short time, and from interested, and probably sinister motives, to instruct among the natives. In 1801, a Moravian mission was established at what is now called Springplace, and one or two excellent men have, since that period, resided there. But, their means having been limited, their influence could not be extensive. Very commendable exertions, in support of a school among the Cherokees, were also made, for a few years subsequent to 1803, by the Rev. Gideon Blackburn.

Excepting these efforts, there was, until the year 1816, nothing done for the Cherokees by the Christian church, nothing by the civilized world. They inhabited a country, which is described as susceptible of the highest cultivation. But most imperfect was their agriculture. They possessed a language, that is said to be more precise and powerful, than any, into which learning has poured richness of thought, or genius breathed the enchantments of fancy and eloquence. But they had no literature. Not a book existed in the language. The fountains of knowledge were unopened. The mind made no progress.

After these statements, the reader will be prepared to credit what will be said, in the progress of this memoir, respecting Catharine's intellectual condition, when she first came under the care of the missionaries.

It is pleasing to observe here, that her moral character was ever irreproachable. This is the more remarkable, considering the looseness of manners then prevalent among the females of her nation, and the temptations to which she was exposed, when, during the war with the Creek Indians, the army of the United States was stationed near her father's residence. Were it proper to narrate some well authenticated facts, with reference to this part of her history, the mind of the reader would be filled with admiration of her heroic virtue, and especially of the protecting care of Providence. Once she even forsook her home, and fled into the wild forest, to preserve her character unsullied.[2]

These occurrences took place before the establishment of a school at Brainerd, while Catharine was young, ignorant of the world, without any clear views of morality, and destitute of the knowledge and love of God. Strange that so great a sense of character should then have influenced her resolutions! But she was a chosen vessel of mercy, and a hand, which she then knew not, was doubtless extended for her preservation.

Early in the autumn of 1816, a missionary, sent by the American Board of Commissioners for Foreign Missions, made his appearance in a general Council of the Cherokees, and offered to establish schools among them. His offer was

---

[2] "I was pleased to find," says a friend, "that General Jackson, (who commanded in the war with the Creeks,) had a high opinion of Catharine. In the course of our conversation he remarked, *She was a woman of Roman virtue, and above suspicion.*"

favourably received. After consultation, a principal chief came forward, took him by the hand, and said: "You have appeared in our full Council. We have listened to what you have said, and understand it. We are glad to see you. We wish to have the schools established, and hope they will be a great advantage to the nation." This missionary was the Rev. Cyrus Kingsbury, who, after commencing and aiding in the formation of the first establishment of the Board among the Cherokees, took up his residence among the Choctaws, was the chief agent in forming the stations of Elliot and Mayhew, and is now the superintendent of the Choctaw mission.

The place selected for the first school, was then called Chickamaugah; but it subsequently received the name of Brainerd, in memory of David Brainerd, that devoted friend and benefactor of the American Indians, who stands pre-eminent among modern missionaries.[3] Early in the following spring, Mr. Moody Hall and Mr. Loring S. Williams, with their wives, arrived as assistant missionaries; and, soon after their arrival, a school was opened, with fair prospects of success.

Information of these proceedings soon spread through the nation. It came to the ears of Catharine, then living at the distance of a hundred miles, and excited in her a desire to attend the school. She besought her parents to send her, and they granted her request. Accordingly, on the 9th of July 1817, when she was about seventeen or eighteen years of age, she became a member of the missionary school at Brainerd.

---

[3] Brainerd is situated within the chartered limits of Tennessee, on the Chickamaugah creek; two miles north of the line of Georgia; seven miles south-east of Tennessee river; two hundred and fifty north-west of Augusta in Geo.; one hundred and fifty south-east of Nashville, and one hundred and ten south-west of Knoxville, both in Tennessee.

MEMOIR OF

CHAPTER II.

FROM HER ENTERING THE SCHOOL AT BRAINERD, UNTIL HER REMOVAL BY HER PARENTS.

Her appearance, when she entered the school.—Her diligence and progress.—Her religious knowledge.—Character of her teachers.—Her conversion, and solicitude for her people.—Instance of earnest prayer.—Prospect of her removal.—Her baptism.—Temporary absence.—Admission to the church.—The early success at Brainerd uncommon.—The chief obstacles to success among the Indians.—Visit of the Treasurer of the American Board.—His account of the school, and description of Catharine.—She is removed from Brainerd.—Is visited by one of the missionaries.—Letters to her friends.

CATHARINE was of the middle stature, erect, of comely features, and blooming complexion; and, even at this time, she was easy in her manners, and modest and prepossessing in her demeanour.

"It was, however, manifest," says Mr. Kingsbury, "that, with all her gentleness and apparent modesty, she had a high opinion of herself, and was fond of displaying the clothing and ornaments, in which she was arrayed. At our first interview, I was impressed with the idea, that her feelings would not easily yield to the discipline of our schools, especially to that part of it, which requires manual labour of the scholars. This objection I freely stated to her, and requested that, if she felt any difficulty on the subject, she would see admission to some other school. She replied, that she had no objection to our regulations. I advised her to take the subject into consideration, and to obtain what information she could, relative to the treatment of the scholars, and if she then felt a desire to become a member of the school, we would receive her.

"She joined the school, and the event has shewn, that it was of the Lord, to the end that his name might be glorified. I have often reflected, with adoring gratitude and thankfulness, on the good providence, which conducted that interesting young female to Brainerd, and which guided her inquiring and anxious mind to the Saviour of sinners."

Sometime before this, it is not known precisely how long, while residing at the house of a Cherokee friend, she had learned to speak the English language, and had acquired, also, a knowledge of the letters of the alphabet. She could even read in words of one syllable. These acquisitions, which were of no particular service at the time they were made, are to be noticed with gratitude to God, as the probable means of leading her to Brainerd. They excited desires, which she could gratify no where else.

Her teachers declare, that, from her first admission to the school, she was attentive to her learning, industrious in her habits, and remarkably correct in her deportment. From reading in words of one syllable, she was able, in sixty days, to read intelligibly in the Bible, and, in ninety days, could read as well as most persons of common education. After writing over four sheets of paper, she could use the pen with accuracy and neatness, even without a copy.

From the testimony of different persons it appears, that, when she entered the school, her knowledge on religious subjects was exceedingly vague and defective. Her ideas of God extended little further than the contemplation of him as a great Being, existing somewhere in the sky; and her conceptions of a future state were quite undefined. Of the Saviour of the world, she had no knowledge. She supposed, that the Cherokees were a different race from the whites, and therefore had no concern in the white people's religion; and it was some time before she could be convinced, that Jesus Christ came into the world to die for the Cherokees. She has been known, also, to remark, subsequently to her conversion, that she was much afraid, when she first heard of religion; for she thought Christians could have no pleasure in this world, and that, if she became religious, she too should be rendered unhappy. How much her opinions and sentiments on this subject were, in a short time, changed, will abundantly appear as we proceed.

That the reader may be duly sensible of the singleness of heart and Christian devotedness of the men, under whose instruction this interesting female had placed herself, he is informed, that, not long after her introduction to them, they adopted the following resolution, which developes an economical principle, carried through all the missions to the Indians, under the direction of the American Board of Commissioners for Foreign Missions.—"That, as God in his providence has called us to labour in the great and good work of building up his kingdom among the Aborigines of this country, a work peculiarly arduous, and which will be attended with much expense; and above all, considering that we have solemnly devoted ourselves, and all that we have, to the prosecution of this work; we declare it to be our cordial, deliberate, and fixed resolution, that, so far as it respects our future labours, or any compensation for them, we will have no private interests distinct from the great interests of this institution. And, that if it meets the views of the Prudential Committee, we will receive no other compensation for our services, than a comfortable supply of food and clothing for ourselves and families, and such necessary expenses as our peculiar circumstances may require; observing at all times that frugality and economy, which our duty to the Christian public and the great Head of the Church demands."

Catharine had been in the school but a very few months, before divine truth began to exert an influence upon her mind. This was manifested in an increased desire to become acquainted with the Christian religion, and in a greater sobriety of manners. A tenderness of spirit, moreover, was, at the same time, observed in several others.

Such was the state of things, when the Rev. Elias Cornelius, then acting as an agent of the American Board, made his first visit to Brainerd. His conversation and preaching had considerable effect on the Cherokees, and on the white people in the neighbourhood of the station. On the last Sabbath of his preaching, which was the first Sabbath in November 1817, four persons were much affected during the service, among whom was Catharine. It is proper to add, that she did not seem, at any time, to be greatly influenced by a fear of the punishment threatened against sin. Her chief object of solicitude seemed rather to be, that she might know the will of God, and do it. She appeared to seek the kingdom of heaven with great earnestness, and spent much time in reading the Scriptures, singing, and prayer, and was often affected to tears. Her whole deportment, as a member of the mission family, is represented as having been unexceptionable.

In December, she indulged a hope, that she had been pardoned and accepted, through the Lord Jesus Christ. And it is no small proof of the excellent practical tendency of her religion, that, of her own accord, she very soon began to pray with her associates, and to assist in teaching the Lord's Prayer and the catechism to the younger girls in the school.

The Rev. William Chamberlain, now residing at a missionary station called Willstown, not far from the place of her nativity, states, that, after the interesting period just mentioned, her desires for the salvation of her people, were strong and ardent. She wept and prayed for them in secret places, as well as in the company of her female friends at their weekly prayer-meetings. Among the rest, the case of her brother David, then on the Arkansas river, was specially interesting. One morning, having retired to the neighbouring woods for devotion, she became so deeply engaged in prayer for this dear brother, that the time passed insensibly, and she remained in her sacred retreat till the sun was near setting. She had been favoured with unusual nearness of access to her heavenly Father, and returned home with an humble confidence, that He would fully answer her prayers. After David had gone to New England to complete his education, having previously given satisfactory evidence of piety, she related these facts to a confidential friend, and said she wished to remember them with gratitude.

Catharine is regarded as the first, who was hopefully converted from among the Indians, by means of the missionaries sent out by the American Board of Missions. It may well be supposed, therefore, considering her amiable manners and promising character, that she was dear to them all. How painful, then, must have been any prospect of her removal into the western wilderness, where she would behold no pious example, and hear no monitory voice; and this, too, at the commencement of her Christian career, before her religious knowledge and habits were matured.

At the commencement of the year 1818, her father came to take her home. He expressed entire satisfaction with the treatment, which she had received at the school; but said he contemplated removing beyond the Mississippi, and wished to have her with him. This intimation was not less painful to Catharine, than it was to the missionaries; but it came under circumstances, which seemed to demand an acquiescence. "Perhaps," said her teachers and spiritual guides, "the Lord is taking her from us, that she may be more useful in promoting his cause in some other place." We shall see, ere long, that they ultimately found occasion to give praise to God, not only on account of the brief separation, which now took place, but also for the more painful separation, which happened in the latter part of the same year.

Catharine desired to receive, before her departure, the seal of the covenant of grace, in the holy ordinance of baptism. As no reasonable doubt could be entertained of her piety, her request was cheerfully granted. On the 25th of January, Mr. Kingsbury preached from Gal. iii, 28, on the fellowship of those, who are in Christ, of whatever colour, or nation. The assembly was unusually large and solemn. After the sermon and a prayer, the sacred ordinance was administered to the deeply affected convert. She was the first Indian baptized by the missionaries of the Board. This event occurred about eight months after the opening of the school at Brainerd. Since then, about one hundred adult Cherokees have received the same ordinance, preparatory to admission to the visible church.

The month of February was spent by Catharine at her father's house. But, circumstances conspiring to prevent an immediate execution of the purpose to remove to the Arkansas country, she was, to the no small satisfaction of herself and the mission family, permitted to revisit Brainerd, and continue there a few months longer, before commencing her undesired journey. While at home, she had been closely questioned, with respect to her religious faith, by some irreligious white people. They endeavoured, though in vain, to perplex her mind, by objections against the Scriptures. But her parents were pleased, that she had learned so many good things, and expressed a desire to be themselves instructed.

Her return furnished an opportunity for admitting her to full communion in the visible Church of Christ. On the 29th of March, about two months after her baptism, she, with others, ratified a solemn covenant with the Most High, at the sacramental table. Seven of the communicants were Cherokees. The assembly was large, solemn and attentive; and there was reason to believe, that some of the bystanders had a great desire to be with the little company, which commemorated the love of Jesus, particularly one negro woman. This person, being asked how she felt on that occasion, replied, "I felt as if that (meaning the communicants,) was my company, and that they had left me alone in the wicked world." "Our red brethren and sisters," say the missionaries, "declared, that their joys, while at the table, exceeded every thing they had before conceived."

It has not been common for missionary stations among Pagans, to be favoured so early, as was Brainerd, with the converting influences of the Spirit of God. Generally, in these latter days, the faith and patience of a missionary, under such circumstances, have been considerably tried, before he has seen the fruits of his labours; though, in due season, there has seldom failed to be a harvest amply compensating him for all his toils. But among the Indians of North America, who have not incorporated the worst vices of civilized life with their own, the preacher of the Gospel has some peculiar advantages. They possess not, as do most heathen nations, a complicated system of false religion, transmitted from their fathers, which must be overthrown, before the Gospel can prevail. They are, to a great extent, "without a sacrifice, and without an image, and without an ephod, and without a teraphim." There is scarcely any thing among the Indians themselves, to oppose the prevalence of the Gospel, except their unfortified ignorance and depravity. The greatest obstacles to missionary success among them, arise from a foreign influence, industriously, and sometimes powerfully, exerted.

In May, Jeremiah Evarts, Esq., at that time Treasurer of the American Board of Commissioners for Foreign Missions, arrived at Brainerd, on a visit of inspection and superintendence. By extracting two or three passages from a letter, which he then wrote, to Dr. Worcester, Corresponding Secretary of the Board, the reader will have an interesting view of the internal economy of the missionary establishment, with which Catharine was connected.

"It was on Friday evening, the 8th inst., just after sun-set, that I alighted at the mission-house. The path, which leads to it from the main-road, passes through an open wood, which is extremely beautiful at this season of the year. The mild radiance of the setting sun, the unbroken solitude of the wilderness, the pleasantness of the forest with all its springing and blossoming vegetation, the object of my journey, and the nature and design of the institution, which I was about to visit, conspired to render the scene solemn and interesting, and to fill the mind with tender emotions.

"Early in the evening, the children of the school, being informed that one of their northern friends, whom they had been expecting, had arrived, eagerly assembled in the hall, and were drawn up in ranks and particularly introduced. They are neither shy, nor forward in their manners. To a stranger they appear not less interesting than other children of the same age; but, if he considers their circumstances and prospects, incomparably more so.

"At evening prayers, I was forcibly struck with the stillness, order, and decorum of the children, and with the solemnity of the family worship. A portion of Scripture was read, with Scott's practical observations; a hymn was sung, in which a large portion of the children united; and Mr. Hoyt led the devotions of the numerous family. If all the members of the Board could hear the prayers, which are daily offered in their behalf at this station, (and I presume at all others under their superintendence;) and if all patrons and contributors could hear the thanks, which are returned to God for their liberality; and especially if they could see a large circle of children, lately rescued from heathenism, kneeling with apparent seriousness, and engaging in the solemnities of Christian worship, one of them [Catharine Brown] already a hopeful convert, and others thoughtful and inquiring;—if all these things could be seen, one may safely predict, that the exertions and sacrifices of the friends of missions would be increased four-fold. These things are not the less real, however, because they cannot be seen by every friend to the cause."

The Rev. Ard Hoyt, mentioned in the above extracts, joined the mission in the January preceding, and, in June, succeeded Mr. Kingsbury as superintendent of the Cherokee mission, the latter having removed to the Choctaw nation.

A farther extract from the letter of Mr. Evarts will not only confirm much, that has already been said respecting Catharine, but will add some other particulars.

"Her parents are half-breeds, who have never learnt to speak English; yet if you were to see her at a boarding-school in

New England, as she ordinarily appears here, you would not distinguish her from well-educated females of the same age, either by her complexion, features, dress, pronunciation, or manners. If your attention were directed to her particularly, you would notice a more than ordinary modesty and reserve. If you were to see her in a religious meeting of pious females, you would not distinguish her, unless by her more than common simplicity and humility. When she joined the school in July last, (having come more than one hundred miles for that sole purpose,) she could read in syllables of three letters, and was seventeen years old. From her superior manners and comely person she had probably attracted more attention, than any other female in the nation. She was vain, and excessively fond of dress, wearing a profusion of ornaments in her ears. She can now read well in the Bible, is fond of reading other books, and has been particularly pleased with the Memoirs of Mrs. Newell. Last fall she became serious, is believed to have experienced religion in the course of the autumn, and was baptized in January. Since that time, she has been constantly in the family; and all the female members of it have the most intimate knowledge of her conduct, and receive a frank disclosure of her feelings. It is their unanimous opinion, that she gives uncommon evidence of piety. At meetings for social prayer and religious improvement, held by them on every Thursday afternoon and Sabbath evening, Catharine prays in her turn, much to the gratification of her sisters in Christ. Her prayers are distinguished by great simplicity as to thought and language, and seem to be the filial aspirations of the devout child. Before Mrs. Chamberlain took charge of the girls, Catharine had, of her own accord, commenced evening prayer with them just as they were retiring to rest. Sometime after this practice had been begun, it was discovered by one of the missionaries, who, happening to pass by the cabin where the girls lodge, overheard her pouring forth her desires in very affecting and appropriate language. On being inquired of respecting it, she simply observed, that she had prayed with the girls, because she thought it was her duty. Yet this young woman, whose conduct might now reprove many professing Christians, who have been instructed in religion from their infancy, only ten months ago had never heard of Jesus Christ, nor had a single thought whether the soul survived the body, or not. Since she became religious, her trinkets have gradually disappeared, till only a single drop remains in each ear. On hearing the pious females have, in many instances, devoted their ornaments to the missionary cause, she has determined to devote hers also. In coming to this determination, she acted without influence from the advice of others."[4]

Time fled rapidly away, in pious employments and in Christian intercourse, and brought the long expected, much dreaded separation. It shall be described in the words of those, who, next to the interesting sufferer, felt it most.

"November 4. The parents of Catharine Brown called on us. They are on their way to the Agency. The old grey-headed man, with tears in his eyes, said he must go over the Mississippi. The white people would not suffer him to live here. They had stolen his cattle, horses, and hogs, until he had very little left. He expected to return from the Agency, in about ten days, and should then want Catharine to go home, and prepare to go with him to Arkansas. We requested him to leave his daughter with us yet a little while, and go to the Arkansas without her; and we would soon send her to him, with much more knowledge than she now has. To this he would not consent; but signified a desire, that some of us would go along with him. It is a great trial to think of sending this dear sister away with only one year's tuition; but we fear she must go. The Lord can and will order otherwise, if on the whole, it is for the best."

While her parents were gone to the Agency, Catharine made a farewell visit to Springplace, the seat of the Moravian mission, about thirty-five miles from Brainerd.

The feelings, with which she parted from Mr. and Mrs. Gambold, the venerable missionaries there, were such as might

---

[4] Panoplist, vol. xiv. p. 344.

be expected, from her high regard for their characters, and her prospect of never seeing them again. She returned to Brainerd on the 9th; and, on the 20th, the missionaries thus describe her removal.

"We had a very affecting scene, in the departure of our sister Catharine. Her father and mother, returning from the Agency to go to the Arkansas, stopped yesterday for the purpose of taking her with them. She knew that she needed more information to be prepared to go alone into the wilderness, and intreated them to leave her with us a little longer. She is their only daughter; and they would not consent on any terms. The struggle was very severe. She wept and prayed, and promised to come to them, as soon as she had finished her literary education, and acquired some further knowledge of the Christian religion. We engaged that she should be provided for while here, and assisted in going to them. He mother said, she could not live, if Catharine would not now go with them. Catharine replied, that to her it would be more bitter than death to leave us, and go where there were no missionaries. He father became impatient, and told her, if she would not mind him, and go with them now, he would disown her forever; but if she would now go, as soon as missionaries came to the Arkansas, (and he expected they would be there soon,) she might go and live with them as longs as she pleased. He wished her to have more learning.

"Never before had this precious convert so severe a trial; and never, perhaps, did her graces shine so bright. She sought for nothing but to know her duty, and asked for a few minutes to be by herself undisturbed. She returned, and said she would go. After she had collected and put up her clothing, the family were assembled, a parting hymn was sung, and a prayer offered. With mingled emotions of joy and grief, we commended her to the grace of God, and they departed.

"Precious babe in Christ ! a few months ago brought out of the dark wilderness; here illuminated by the word and Spirit of God; and now to be sent back into the dark and chilling shades of the forest, without one fellow traveller, with whom she can say, 'Our Father!' O ye, who with delight sit under the droppings of the sanctuary, and enjoy the communion of saints, remember Catharine in your prayers."

Thus was she removed from a place, endeared to her by some of the most pleasing associations of her life, and she departed, expecting to return no more. A day of sorrow must it have been to the members of the school, whose warmest attachment she had most effectually secured. The chief consolation of her religious friends was, that the whole had been ordered by infinite Wisdom.

Early in the following month, information was received at Brainerd, that two children, who had been taken captive by the Cherokees from the Osage tribe of Indians, were in the lower part of the nation, and that one of them was supposed to be the sister of *Lydia Carter*, the interesting "Little Osage Captive,"[5] who was then a member of the school. There being some reason to believe, that the man, in whose possession they were, might be induced to surrender them to the care of the missionaries, Mr. Hoyt, accompanied by his son, set out in quest of the unfortunate children. They travelled between two and three hundred miles, and encountered many hardships on their way. But, though they found the children, and ascertained that one was indeed the sister of Lydia, they failed in their great object. The man, who professed to be the owner of the children, would not relinquish them.[6]

The journey was not, however, in vain. Mr. Hoyt had the happiness of meeting with Catharine, at her father's house. This occurrence is thus noticed, in the journal of the mission.

"In this tour, father Hoyt spent two nights and a day at the house of Catharine Brown's father. He was received with great cordiality by the whole family; and Catharine's joy was so great,

---

[5] The little girl, a narrative of whom was published, in 1822, by the Rev. Elias Cornelius, now Pastor of the Tabernacle Church in Salem, Mass.

[6] The girl was never obtained by the missionaries; but the boy was afterwards placed under their care, through the kindness of Col. Meigs, the United States Agent, and through the benevolent enterprise of Mr. John Ross, a promising Cherokee young man. The boy was named *John Osage Ross*, in honour of Mr. Ross.

that he says, 'I felt myself more than paid for the fatigues of the whole journey, by the first evening's opportunity.' Catharine said, it had been very dark times with her, since she left Brainerd. All around her were engaged for the riches and pleasures of the world; and because she could not unite with them, as formerly, they were telling her, they supposed she thought herself very good now; that she expected to go to heaven alone; &c. Her greatest burden was, a fear that she should be drawn away from the right path, and at length be left to do like those around her. She felt herself too weak to leave the society and instruction of Christians, and go into the world alone."

While Mr. Hoyt was at her father's, he preached to a small audience of Cherokees, and one Indian woman was so much affected, that she wept during the whole service. After the departure of Mr. Hoyt, this woman sent for Catharine to read and explain the Bible to her, and to pray with her, which was repeatedly done. There is reason to believe, that a salutary and abiding impression was produced; for, after Catharine's return to Brainerd, this poor female came all the way, a distance of more than a hundred miles, to hear, as she said, more about the Saviour.

This chapter will be closed with two letters from Catharine to her friends, which are the earliest, of which her biographer has any knowledge. And this occasion is taken to remark, that nearly all the letters, which will find a place in this memoir, were written from the overflowings of her heart to persons with whom she was intimately acquainted, and hence with little study, or effort. The greater part of them have never before been published. They are generally copied from the originals, which are in a plain, intelligible running hand, and the orthography is very seldom incorrect. Alterations in the sense, are never made; and corrections in the grammar, but rarely.

The first of the letters was written in the anticipation of her dreaded removal from her Christian friends, sixteen months from her first coming to Brainerd.

CATHARINE BROWN

TO MRS. WILLIAMS, AT ELLIOT.

Brainerd, Nov. 1, 1818.

My dearly beloved Sister,

I HAVE been wishing to write to you ever since you left us. You can hardly tell how my heart ached when I parted with you, expecting never to see you again in this world; but when I remembered that you were in the hands of the Lord, and that he would dispose of you as he pleased, it gave me joy equal to my sorrow.

O how I rejoiced, to think that you were going to carry the glad tidings of salvation to a people who had never heard of the dear Saviour. I do hope and pray that the Lord will bless your labours among them, as he has here.

We were very lonesome when you left us, especially at our prayer meeting; but I hope our hearts were united in love. I was very sorry to hear that you were sick; but it rejoiced me to hear that you were recovering, O, my dear sister, I will join with you in praising the Lord for his goodness in restoring you to health. I shall never forget you, or your kind endeavours to bring me to a knowledge of the Saviour. Sometimes I feel the love of God shed abroad in my heart, and feel as if I should be willing to give up every thing in this world to Christ. O how good is it to enjoy the presence of God; O that I might always enjoy it: but my heart is so bad and so prone to leave the God I love, that I am afraid he will leave me. O my dear sister, do pray for me.

All the Cherokee brothers and sisters are well. Three of the scholars, viz. Lydia Lowry, Alice, and Peggy Wilson, we hope have obtained an interest in the Saviour. Mr. Wilson came here, and wished to take his daughters on a visit to Mr. Brown's. Nearly a week after, he sent word that he was not going to send them back to school again. We felt very much grieved to hear it.

I expect my father here every day. I do not know whether I shall go to the Arkansas, or not. I feel grieved when I think of leaving my Christian friends, and of going far from all religious people, into a wild howling wilderness, where no star shines to guide my wandering feet to the Babe of Bethlehem; where no warning voice is heard to keep me in the straight path that leads to heaven. When I look to that dark region, I start back; but when I think of my two brothers there, and my dear parents, who are soon to go, I feel reluctant to stay behind, and leave them to perish alone.

Tell Mr. Williams and Mr. Kingsbury, that I remember them most affectionately, and also all the dear brothers and sisters at Yello Busha.

From your loving sister,

CATHARINE BROWN.

TO MR. AND MRS. CHAMBERLAIN, AT BRAINERD.

Fort Deposit, Dec. 12, 1818.

My dearly beloved Brother and Sister Chamberlain,

I JUST sit down to address you with my pen. But is this all? Am I so soon called to bid you adieu, and see your faces no more in this world? O my beloved friends, you know not the love I bear to that blessed spot, where I have spent so many happy hours with you, but it is past never to return.

Dear friends, I weep; my heart is full; tears flow from my eyes while I write; and why is it so? Do I murmur? God forbid. Ought I not to praise the Lord for what I have received, and trust Him for every thing? O yes, his ways are best, and he has graciously promised, that "all things shall work together for good to them that love him." But do I love him? Have I that love to him, which will enable me to keep all his commandments? Do I love him with all my heart? O that the Lord would search me, and lead me in the way of eternal life.

Since I left you, I have led a very lonesome life, and not heard the Gospel preached but once; that is, when father Hoyt was here, and Milo. They came here on Tuesday evening. I was sitting in my room, and heard a knocking at the door. I bid them come in; and who but Milo appeared. I inquired if any body was with him. He said his father was at the door. That rejoiced me very much, and I enjoyed very much while they were here. Blessed be God for sending them here to instruct us.

I am here amongst a wicked set of people, and never hear prayers, nor any godly conversation. O my dear friends, pray for me: I hope you do. There is not a day passes but I think of you, and the kindness I received during the time I staid with you. It is not my wish to go to the Arkansas; but God only knows what is best for me. I shall not attempt to tell you what I have felt since I left you, and the tears I have shed when I called to mind the happy moments we passed in singing the praises of God. However, I bear it as well as I possibly can, trusting in our dear Saviour, who will never leave nor forsake them, that put their trust in him.

It may be possible, that I may see you once more; it would be a great happiness to me if I don't go to the Arkansas; perhaps I may; but if I should go, it is not likely we shall meet in this world again:—but you will excuse me, for my heart feels what I cannot express with my pen. When I think and see the poor thoughtless Cherokees going on in sin, I cannot help blessing God, that he has led me in the right path to serve him.

Father will start to the Arkansas about some time after Christmas; but, I am not certain that I shall go.

I thank you for your kind letters. Do write to me every opportunity.

I shall conclude with my love to all my brothers and sisters at Brainerd. Sister Flora, do kiss all the children for me. I shall expect letters from all the little girls. O may we meet at last in the kingdom of our blessed Saviour, never more to part. Farewell, my dear brother and sister, farewell.

From you affectionate sister in Christ.

CATHARINE BROWN.

CHAPTER III.

FROM HER RETURN TO BRAINERD, UNTIL SHE TAKES CHARGE OF A SCHOOL AT CREEK-PATH.

Benefits resulting from her being taken from the school.—Her return.—Letters.—Her brother David a member of the school.—His conversion.—Catharine and David visit their sick father.—A school established near Mr. Brown's.—Account of John Arch.—Efforts of Catharine and David at Brainerd.—The latter goes to New England.—His subsequent history.—A female teacher wanted at Creek-Path.—Catharine undertakes this service.—Letters.

THOSE, who will but observe, may often witness very affecting instances of the particular and merciful providence, which God exercises towards his children in this world. Both the removal and the return of Catharine may be regarded as such instances.

What was the precise influence upon her own character, of her being taken from Brainerd, cannot be determined; though there is little doubt but her faith and patience were, by this means, increased. But the consequences of her removal to others, are more obvious. It led the way to the formation of schools, and to the stated preaching of the Gospel, at Creek-Path, the place of her father's residence, and to the hopeful conversion of nearly all her family; thus illustrating the maxim, that our greatest blessings may spring from our severest afflictions.

Her return was scarcely expected by the missionaries, when, on the 23d of May 1819, her father brought her again to Brainerd, and committed her to their care, until her education should be completed, intending to remove immediately, with the remainder of his family, beyond the Mississippi. This purpose, as has been previously intimated, was not executed. Mr. Brown did not proceed to the Arkansas country until more than four years after this time, and not till the beloved daughter, for whose society he was so desirous, had been laid in the dust. The causes of this delay are unknown to the author of this memoir.

Catharine ascribed the change in the intentions of her parents respecting her, wholly to the special providence of Him, who heareth prayer. The appointed time for their departure drew near. She was convinced that it was not best for her to go. Her continual intercessions were, that her parents might be induced to leave her behind. And her prayers were answered. After one of her seasons of private devotion, she returned to her family, with a delightfully confident hope, that God had listened to her requests; and, as she entered the room where her parents were sitting, she found they had been consulting on the expediency of sending her back to Brainerd; and had actually resolved upon her return. This was just half a year from the period of her removal from that consecrated place.

On this occasion, the missionaries very naturally exclaim;—"How unsearchable are the ways of God! We thought it a very afflicting providence that this lamb should be snatched from the fold of Christ, to go, as we thought, where she would be exposed to be devoured by wolves; and were ready to say in our hearts, when her father required her to go with him, 'not so.' But in this very way, God has given her an opportunity to set an example of filial obedience, by submitting to the authority of a father, in a most painful requisition, and of manifesting her love to the Saviour, in her willingness to forsake all for him; and, at the same time, has granted her the object of her pious and fervent desire."

MEMOIR OF

With how much delight she revisited the scenes of her first aspirations after God and heaven, will appear in a letter, which was written a few days after her arrival at Brainerd.

TO MR. AND MRS. HALL, AT KNOXVILLE.

Brainerd, May 30, 1819.

My dear Brother and Sister,

WITH pleasure I spend a few moments in writing to you this evening, to tell you of my safe arrival on the 23d of this month. O how great was the joy that I felt, when meeting the dear family at Brainerd, with whom I have long desired to be. Yes, dear brother and sister, God has returned me back once more, where I can be with Christian friends, and get more instruction. If it is the Lord's will, I hope to stay here two years longer. O that I might improve the great privileges, which I now enjoy.

It appears strange to me, that I am not more interested in the cause of Christ, when he has done so much for me. But I will now give myself up entirely to Him. I should be willing to leave every thing for God, and to undergo any sufferings, if it would but make me humble, and would be for his glory.

My heart bleeds for my people, who are on the brink of destruction. O pray for me, my dear brother and sister. I long to see you and your little one. I am your affectionate sister,

CATHARINE BROWN.

Of her employments, from this time till the end of the year, the documents, on which the principal reliance is placed, contain no important notices. Doubtless she was occupied in making useful acquisitions; and, so far as her duties as a member of the school would permit, in communicating the knowledge she had acquired to others.

Two or three letters may properly be inserted here.

CATHARINE BROWN

TO MR. AND MRS. WILLIAMS.

Brainerd, July 5, 1819.

My dear Brother and Sister Williams,

ALTHOUGH I have long omitted answering your affectionate letters, my heart has been often with you. Yes, dear brother and sister, I do not forget you, and all the pleasant meetings we had together, when you were here. But pain is mixed with pleasure, when I think they are gone, no more to return! When I remember the kind instruction I received from you, before you left this place, my heart swells with gratitude. I feel much indebted to you, but more particularly to that God, who sent you here to instruct the poor ignorant Indians in the way that leads to everlasting life. Oh, my dear friends, may the Lord ever bless you, and make you the instrument of doing great good where he has called you.

You may pass through many trials; but remember, beloved brother and sister, all our trials here will only make us richer there, when we arrive at our home. A few more days, and then I hope our weary souls will be at rest in our Saviour's kingdom, where we shall enjoy His blessed presence forever.

When I wrote you before, I expected to go to the Arkansas, and never to see this place again. But the Lord has in mercy ordered it otherwise. He has permitted me to live with the dear missionaries here again, though my parents could not bear to think of leaving me behind. My mother said, if I remained here, she did not expect to see me again in this world. Indeed, she wished she had never sent me to this school, and that I had never received religious instruction. I told her, if she was a Christian she would not feel so. She would be willing to give me, and all she had, up to Christ. I told her I did not wish to stay on account of my own pleasure; but that I wished to get more instruction, so that it might be for her good, as well as for mine.

I felt very sorry for my poor parents. I thought it was my duty to go in obedience to their commands, and commit myself to the will of God. I knew the Lord could change the hearts of my parents.

They are now perfectly willing, that I should stay here two years longer. I left them in March. They expected to set out in that month for the Arkansas. They had already prepared for the journey. But the Lord has so ordered, that they have concluded not to go until next fall. I don't know whether they will go then. I hope you will pray for them, and also for me, that I may be useful to my dear people. My heart bleeds for their immortal souls. O that I might be made the means of turning many souls from darkness unto marvelous light.

My dear brother and sister, I love you much, and feel that the time is short when we shall sit down with our Saviour, and experience that love which no words can describe.

Give my love to my dear brother and sister Kingsbury, and also to all the dear missionaries there. From your affectionate sister in Christ,   CATHARINE BROWN.

P.S. Please to accept this small present for my little darlings; and learn them to say, "Aunt Catharine."[7]

TO MR. MOODY HALL, AT TALONEY.[8]

Brainerd, Oct. 25, 1819.

A FEW moments of this day shall be spent in writing to my dear brother. It seems a long time, since you left us. I long to

---

[7] Any person who had witnessed the separation of Mrs. Williams from her Cherokee friends, when she and her husband left Brainerd and set out for the Choctaw mission, in May 1818, could well understand the affectionate expressions in this letter. When the boat was ready to proceed, and the hour of parting had arrived; when Mr. Cornelius had made the last prayer, and the last hymn had been sung; Catharine was among those who seemed ready to sink under a burden of grief too great to be borne. Mrs. Williams had always been peculiarly dear to her from their first acquaintance, and, like an older sister, had guided her youthful steps in the paths of peace.
[8] Now called Carmel.

see you. I long to hear from you. I hope the Lord is with you this day, that you enjoy the presence of our dear Redeemer. My sincere desire and earnest prayer to the throne of grace, is, that your labours may be blessed, and that God would make you the instrument of saving many souls from eternal destruction.

O how I feel for my poor Cherokee brethren and sisters, who do not know the blessed Jesus, that died for us, and do not enjoy the blessings that I do. How thankful I ought to be to God, that I have ever been brought to the light of the Gospel, and was not left to wander in darkness. O I hope the time is at hand, when all the heathen shall know God, whom to know is life everlasting.

My dear brother, may we be faithful to our Master, knowing that in due season we shall reap, if we faint not. Our pilgrimage will shortly be ended, and all our trials will be over. Do not forget me in your daily prayers, for I need very much the prayers of God's children. My heart is prone to leave my God, whom I love. From your unworthy sister in Christ, CATHARINE BROWN.

TO MR. AND MRS. HALL,
On their removal from Brainerd.

Brainerd, Nov.—,1819.

How solemn, my dear brother and sister, is the idea, that we must soon part. Perhaps the next time we meet will be in eternity, before the bar of God. O my dear brother and sister, if we are prepared to meet our God in peace, we shall surely be happy. But, my beloved friends, how can I be permitted to meet you in heaven! My heart is so prone to sin against God, that I am sometimes afraid he will leave me. Forget not to pray, that all these doubts may be removed from me, and that my soul may be washed in the blood of Jesus Christ.

I love you much, and feel that the time is short when we shall sit down with our Saviour. Farewell, my dear brother and sister. May the Lord go with you. From your sister

CATHARINE.

In the same month, in which the last letter was written, we find David Brown, the brother of Catharine, employed, in connexion with another young Indian named John Arch, to assist the Rev. Mr. Butrick, one of the missionaries at Brainerd, in preparing a Cherokee spelling-book, which was afterwards printed for the use of the schools. Of course, David had previously entered the school. And we may safely conclude that she, who had prayed so earnestly for him, when he was absent, would not fail to exert herself for his spiritual good, when present. Her efforts, in conjunction with those of the missionaries, were not ineffectual. David became thoughtful—deeply impressed—convinced of his sinfulness and his need of salvation by Jesus Christ—and, early in the year 1820, hopes were entertained, that he had become truly pious.

Soon after this, hearing that their father was ill, these young converts from heathenism went home to see him. They remained at home about seven weeks. Catharine says, "David seized his Bible as soon as he reached home, and began to read and interpret to his father and mother, and the other members of the family, exhorting them to attend to it as the word of God, to repent of their sins, which he told them were many and great, and to become the followers of the Lord Jesus Christ." With his father's consent, he maintained the worship of God in the family, morning and evening, and craved a blessing and gave thanks at the table. He also conversed freely with friends and neighbours, boldly professing himself a Christian.

The impression made by this visit, in connexion with the previous efforts of Catharine, was such, that when Mr. Brown, after recovering from his illness, brought his children back to Brainerd, he delivered to the missionaries the following letter, signed by himself and others, headmen and chiefs.

"We, the headmen, chiefs of the Creek-Path town, Cherokee nation, have this day assembled ourselves together for the purpose of devising some plan for the education of our children. We daily witness the good effects arising from education, and therefore are extremely anxious to have a school in our neighbourhood, as the distance from this part of the nation to Chickamaugah is so great as not to suit our convenience. We therefore solicit your aid in carrying our plan into execution. We can raise twenty, or perhaps twenty-five children. You will please write us immediately on the receipt of this. Given under our hands, this 16th of February 1820."

In consequence of this request, the Rev. Daniel S. Butrick, who had acquired some knowledge of the Cherokee language, left Brainerd for Creek-Path, on the 11th of March, and, at a place about two miles from Mr. Brown's residence, the natives having erected a convenient house for the purpose, he soon after opened a school, under very favourable auspices.

Mr. Butrick was accompanied and much assisted by John Arch, a converted Cherokee of good promise, whose name has already been mentioned. This young man was born and bred among the mountains, near the confines of South Carolina, in the most ignorant part of the nation. Happening to be at Knoxville, Tenn. in December 1818, he saw Mr. Hall, who informed him of the school at Chickamaugah. Returning home, he took his gun, and set off in search of the place. After travelling a hundred and fifty miles, he arrived at the station, told the missionaries he had come to attend the school, and offered them his gun, which was his only property, for clothes. We are informed his appearance was so wild and forbidding, that the missionaries hesitated to receive him, especially as he was supposed to be not less than twenty years of age. But he would not be refused. They took him upon trial. It was not long before he discovered an anxious solicitude respecting his soul, and soon gave the most satisfactory evidence of piety. His thirst for knowledge was ardent, and his application and proficiency in learning were gratifying. In ten months he could read and write well. Sometime after he became serious, he was falsely accused, by some one of his schoolmates, of doing an improper act. Conscious of innocence, he could not well brook the charge. That evening and night he was missing, and the next morning it was concluded that he had absconded. But in the course of the forenoon, he made his appearance. On being questioned respecting his absence, he made this reply: "I felt angry, and knew that it was wicked. But I could not suppress it. I therefore went to seek the Saviour, that he might reconcile my heart." It appeared, that he had spent the night in devotional exercises. He was at length admitted to the church, and, from that day to the present, has sustained a good Christian character. He has been much employed as an interpreter, both at the different stations, and in the evangelical labours of the missionaries in various parts of the nation.

While Mr. Butrick was prosecuting his incipient labours at Creek-Path, Catharine and David were employing themselves diligently at Brainerd. Once, in particular, it is recorded, that, after a prayer-meeting, conducted by the missionaries, these two young Cherokees, aided by a pious Indian woman of great age, collected a little group of their people, who had come to spend the Sabbath there, and held a religious conference, with prayer and praise, all in the Cherokee language.

These united labours were, however, interrupted, on the 11th of May, never to be resumed, by the departure of David for the Foreign Mission School in Cornwall, Conn. He left Brainerd only a few days after his admission to the church.

David had been desirous, for some time, of being fitted to preach the Gospel to his countrymen, and was encouraged to aim at such a preparation, first by his sister Catharine, and then by the missionaries. He arrived at Cornwall, sometime in the summer; was connected with that highly favoured school about two years; was then removed to Andover, Mass. where he remained a year, and, without becoming a member of the Theological Institution in that place, enjoyed many of its distinguished advantages. In consequence of the state of his

health, and of the great need of his services among those of his countrymen, who reside in the Arkansas country, he returned to them, early in the year 1824. The addresses, which he delivered in many of our principal towns and cities, on the wrongs and claims and prospects of the American Indians, will not soon be forgotten by those who listened to them.

Since his return, a letter has been received, by the Corresponding Secretary of the American Board, which, coming from one so nearly related to Catharine, and giving an amiable view of her family, will interest the reader.

Point Pleasant, Arkansas, Sept. 20, 1824.

Dear Sir,

LONG before this time, you must have heard of my speedy passage from Washington City to Arkansas, and of my delightful and joyful meeting with my brethren and kindred according to the flesh. My father and mother embraced me with tears. We were unable to converse, for more than an hour: our mutual joy was so great, that we could not speak for some time. My friends ran as far as they could see me, in order to meet me, and embrace me. The scene was somewhat similar to that of Jacob meeting with his beloved son Joseph.

I was glad to find so much religious feeling among my friends. My parents are very useful in this country, by making known to others the way of salvation. Since my arrival I have had no rest. My friends and relatives are so numerous, that I am constantly on a visit. Dwight, and the residence of my brother Webber, I have made my homes. At Dwight I have all my books. On the Sabbath, I interpret English sermons, and sometimes preach myself in the sweet language of *Tsállakee,* [the Cherokee.] Never were there greater prospects of success among the Cherokees, than at present.

I expect to revisit my mother-country soon, on my father's business, and once more to be at Brainerd, and Creek-Path, beneath the tall trees of *Tsu-saw-ya-wa-sah.* In November and

December please to write me at Brainerd, and inform me whether the Board can send us a printer, who is accomplished in his art. Pray send us one.

My fond remembrance to your family. Time and distance can never erase from my bosom the marks of friendship and attention I received in Boston. DAVID BROWN.

About the time of David's departure for New England, Mr. Butrick's school, at Creek-Path, had so increased in the number of its scholars, that there was no more room for the admission of other applicants. The people therefore desired another school. They said, if a female would come to instruct their daughters, they would build a school-house for her. At the same time, it was evident, that a spirit of deep seriousness and anxious inquiry was beginning to prevail among them.

These facts being known at Brainerd, the missionaries thought it their duty to advise Catharine to go and take charge of the contemplated school. In this advice she acquiesced, though not without a painful diffidence of her qualifications for such a service. When it was known to Creek-Path, that she was to take charge of the school, the most enthusiastic joy was occasioned among the people. They seemed to feel, that the preparations could not be made too soon. Not less than fifty Cherokee men, besides negroes and boys, assembled immediately to build a house, which, in two days, was nearly completed according to their stipulation.

Every thing being in readiness, Mr. Brown came for his daughter. She was at Taloney, the missionary station where her friends Mr. and Mrs. Hall resided, and he waited at Brainerd for her return; during which time it was perceived, that the venerable old man was anxiously inquiring after the truth. On the last of May 1820, a little less than two years and eleven months from her first entering the school, as an untaught heathen girl, Catharine bade an affectionate adieu to Brainerd, to take charge of the school for females near her paternal home. The

following entry was made at this time, in the journal of the mission.

"31. Catharine left us, in company with her father, to go to Creek-Path, to teach a school of females.

"How very different the scene from that, which passed here not quite two years since, when her father required her to leave the society of Christians, and to accompany him to the then dark shades of the Arkansas! Now, he does not ask her without our consent; will not take her except by our advice; and she is going, not into the wilderness unprepared to teach, but into a place where divine light has already begun to spring up, prepared, as we think, to instruct others. Yet, it is highly probable, that this removal will not be productive of so much good as the former. So unsearchable are the ways of God, and so incompetent is man to judge. It now appears, that her first removal was the means of sowing the seed, which is now springing up at Creek-Path with such hopeful promise."

The remaining letters written during the period embraced by this chapter, will now be inserted. The first was originally published at the close of the narrative of the "Little Osage Captive."

TO A LADY IN CONNECTICUT.

Brainerd, Jan. 12, 1820.
Dear Sister in Christ,

I THANK you much for your affectionate letter, which I received on the 23d of December. O, how great, how rich is the mercy of our dear Redeemer, who has made us the subjects of his kingdom, and led us, as we trust from death unto life. My dear sister, I can never express my gratitude to God, for his goodness towards me, and my dear people. Surely it is of *his own glorious mercy*, that he is sending to us the Gospel of the Lord Jesus, in this distant land, where the people had long set in darkness, and were perishing for lack of the knowledge of God. Blessed be his holy name! O my sister let us rejoice continually in our Lord and Saviour, and as we have put on Christ, not only by outward profession, but by inward and spiritual union, let us walk worthy of our high and holy vocation, and shew the world, that there is something in true religion. And may the Lord give us strength to do his will, and to follow continually the example of our meek and lowly Jesus. I thank you for the present you sent me, which I received as a token of love. The mission family are all well, and also the dear children. Many of them are serious, and we hope they love and pray to God daily. O that I were more engaged for God, to promote his cause, among these dear children, and my people. I am going soon to visit my parents, which is an hundred miles from here, and expect to stay two months. I hope you will pray for me, that the Lord would bless my visit, and renew the hearts of my dear parents.

Your sincere friend and sister in Christ,
CATHARINE BROWN.

TO MRS. ISABELLA HALL, AT TALONEY.

Brainerd, March 8, 1820.

My dear Sister,

IT is with pleasure I take time this morning to assure you, that my love for you is still as great as ever. You cannot tell how painful it was to me to hear that you had been sick. But we know, that the Lord is good, and that all things will work together for good to those who love him, and put their whole trust in him. O could we see each other, how would we talk, and weep, and sing, and pray together.

But our Heavenly Father has separated us. Perhaps we loved each other more than we loved him, and did not pray to him, and praise him, and thank him, as we ought to have done. And it is not so, dear sister? Did we not neglect our duty, and grow cold and careless, when we were together? Now we are sorry, and the Lord will forgive us. Still, dear sister, we can pray for each other. Think you not that our prayers often meet at the throne of grace? O then let us pray on, and never cease to pray for each other, while he lends us breath; and when we meet in heaven, we shall see him whom our soul loveth.

Let us praise the Lord for what he is doing. My dear brother David is now rejoicing in his blessed Redeemer. He has a great desire to do good among our people. I expect he will leave us, in two or three weeks, for Cornwall, to study divinity, and prepare to preach the Gospel of Jesus Christ. I do hope and pray that the Lord will go with him, and enable him to do much good in the word.

He and myself spent seven weeks with our dear parents, and returned to school the last week. I hope to continue here some time longer, but know not how long. My dear mother feels that she cannot spare me much longer, I wish to learn as much as I can, before I go.

And now, my dear sister, may we both be faithful to our Lord, and do much in the world. And when time with us shall be not more, may we be permitted to meet in that world, where Christians will be collected to sing through eternity the song of Moses and the Lamb.

From your sister
CATHARINE BROWN.

TO HER BROTHER DAVID,
While on his way to New England.

Brainerd, May 16, 1820.

My very dear Brother,

I CANNOT express my feelings this evening, when I read your kind letter. My heart is full. But we know, dear brother, that our Saviour orders all things right. I am very sorry to hear that you have lost your horse. What will you do now? But let us not be troubled about these things. If it is best that you should go on, the Saviour will provide for you in some way. Let us only, my dear brother, put our whole trust in God, and be humble at the feet of Jesus. We can do nothing of ourselves. We are like little children. If we rely on our own strength, we shall fall.

It is impossible for me to express what I felt, the morning you left us. But I thought, that if I should never see you again in this world, I should meet you in a better, where there will be no separation. O how thankful we ought to be to God, who has brought us from darkness into the light of the Gospel.

But many of our dear people are yet deprived of this great privilege. They know not the Saviour, whom we have found so precious. Yes, even our dear parents are yet living without any hope in God. O my brother, let us never cease to pray for them. God will surely hear us, if we ask in faith.

Dear brother, forget me not in your prayers. Your sister C. will never forget you. When you are far from this place, your poor sister C. will be praying for you. Good night, dear brother, till we meet again.

CATHARINE BROWN.

CHAPTER IV.

FROM HER TAKING CHARGE OF A SCHOOL AT CREEK-PATH, UNTIL HER SICKNESS.

Extracts from her diary.—Her school.—Conversion of her parents, and others of the family.—She and her family visit Brainerd.—Letter from the chiefs at Creek Path.— Traits in Catharine's character.—Further extracts from her diary.—Eulogium of her brother John.—She visits Huntsville.—Estimation in which she was there held.— Goes to reside with her parents.—Apprehensions respecting her health.—Goes to Brainerd for medical aid.—Returns.—Letters to different friends.

WE now enter upon the last three, and the most interesting years of Catharine's life, in which we shall behold her in new circumstances; her character more fully developed, and her graces shining with greater lustre.

In order that she may speak for herself as much as possible, that part of her private diary will be inserted, which was saved from the destruction, to which many of her papers were devoted, a little before her sickness. It was obtained from Mrs. Gilbreth, a sister of Catharine, and a faithful copy was transmitted by Mrs. Potter, the wife of the Rev. William Potter, missionary at Creek-Path.

EXTRACTS FROM HER DIARY.

"*Brainerd, May* 30, 1820. Tomorrow morning I shall leave this school, perhaps never to return. It is truly painful to part with my dear Christian friends, those, with whom I have spent many happy hours in the house of worship. I must bid them farewell. This is the place, where I first became acquainted with the dear Saviour. He now calls me to work in his vineyard, and shall I, for the sake of my Christian friends and of my own pleasures, refuse to go, while many of my poor red brothers and sisters are perishing for lack of knowledge? O no. I *will not* refuse to go. I will go wherever the Saviour calls me. I know he will be on my right hand, to grant me all the blessings, that I shall need, and he will direct me how to instruct the dear children, who shall be committed to my care.

"31. This morning I set out from Brainerd, with my dear father. Travelled about twenty miles. Thought much of my beloved Christian friends. Whether I shall ever see them again, is uncertain. The Lord only knows.

"June 2. Have been very sick to day; but, blessed be God, am now a little better. Hope I shall be able to travel tomorrow. The Lord is very kind and merciful to all those, who put their trust in him. Last night I slept on the floor without any bed. Felt quite happy in my situation. Though very sick in body, yet I trust my heart was well.

"5. Have arrived at my father's, but am yet very unwell. Have a bad cold. Am sometimes afraid I shall not be able to teach school at Creek-Path. We slept two nights on the ground with our wet blankets, before we reached our home.

"20. Blessed be God, who has again restored me to health. It is two weeks to-day since I commenced teaching a girl's school. O how much I need wisdom from God. I am a child. I can do nothing. But in God will I trust, for I know there is none else, to whom I can look for help.

"Sept. 5. This day I received a letter from brother David. I rejoice much to hear, that he has arrived safely at Cornwall. May the Lord be with him, and make him useful as long as he lives, and at death may he be received at the right hand of God. This is the prayer of his affectionate sister Catharine."

Before proceeding further with the extracts from the diary, it seems proper to insert some notices not found in that document.

Catharine commenced her school with about twenty scholars, and the number soon increased. Not only the daughters, but the mothers also, manifested a strong desire to receive instruction. Several of her pupils, in consequence of previous tuition, could read in the New Testament, when they came under her care. These it was her delight to lead to a more perfect acquaintance with that sacred volume. But most of the children began with the rudiments of learning. This school she continued three quarters of a year, much to the satisfaction of her scholars, their parents, and the missionaries. She finally relinquished it only because the arrival of Mr. and Mrs. Potter gave her an opportunity to surrender her charge into other hands, and at the same time opened the way for her prosecuting higher studies, with a view to greater usefulness to her people.

The spirit of serious inquiry at Creek Path, to which there was an allusion at the close of the last chapter, increased after the arrival of Catharine, especially among her own kindred. Doubtless she was not backward, with the meekness of humility and with the earnestness of affection, to warn and exhort. And she had the joy of beholding her father, mother, a brother, and two or three sisters, unitedly seeking the pardon of their sins, and that peace, which the world giveth not. After a suitable trial, and due instruction, all these her relatives, with others of their countrymen, publicly professed faith in Christ, and were united to his visible Church.

It is gratifying to be able to remark, that no one of them has hitherto dishonoured the Christian profession, and that all who survive, are believed to be the humble followers of the Lord Jesus. One has "fallen asleep," and of him an affectionate record will be found in the diary of Catharine.

Shortly after the last paragraph extracted from her diary was written, nearly the whole family made a visit to Brainerd. The hearts of the missionaries were made glad, by the sight of this little band; and oh! how must the heart of Catharine have exulted with joy, while she presented her beloved relatives, one after another, as the friends and followers of her blessed Saviour!

It will be remembered that a letter from the Chiefs at Creek-Path, desiring the missionaries to establish a school among them, was inserted in the last chapter. Mr. Brown was now the bearer of another letter from the same chiefs, signed by their Chairman, or Speaker, in which they thus express their approbation of the school, and their good wishes with respect to missionary efforts:

"Friends and Brothers,

"We are glad to inform you, that we are well pleased with Mr. Butrick, who has come forward as a teacher to instruct our people. We believe he does discharge his duty; and we hope his coming will be of great advantage to our people. Our wish is, that you may prosper throughout our nation, in your laudable undertaking. It is out of our power to see you, in any short time, on account of the National Council, and other business we are obliged to attend at this time. It is our wish that the school should continue at this place. Mr. John Brown, sen. will deliver this, who will present you our hands in friendship. We hope we shall see each other before long. We are glad to see our children advancing so well. We conclude with our best respects.

WAU-SAU-SEY, *Bear-meat*, Speaker."

Here some remarks may properly be introduced, on the traits of character, which Catharine exhibited, during a part of the time embraced in her diary. These remarks are taken from the letter of Mrs. Potter, which enclosed that document.

"In the spring of 1821, while making the necessary preparations for a settlement at Creek-Path, Mr. Potter and myself, for two months, made Mr. Brown's house our home. Here we had an opportunity of noticing Catharine's daily deportment, as a member of the domestic circle.

"For sweetness of temper, meekness, gentleness, and forbearance, I never saw one, who surpassed her. To her parents she was uncommonly dutiful and affectionate. Nothing, which could contribute to their happiness, was considered a burden; and her plans were readily yielded to theirs, however great the sacrifice to her feelings. The spiritual interests of the family lay near her heart, and she sometimes spent whole evenings in conversation with them on religious subjects.

"Before our arrival, she had established a weekly prayer-meeting with the female members of the family, which was also improved as an opportunity for reading the word of God, and conversing upon its important truths. Such was her extreme modesty, that she did not make this known to me, until more than a week after my arrival; and the usual period had passed without a meeting. She at length overcame her diffidence, and informed me what their practice had been, in a manner expressive of the most unfeigned humility. These meetings were continued while we remained in the family, and I believe they were highly useful. A monthly prayer-meeting among the sisters of the church was soon after established, in which Catharine took a lively interest; nor did she ever refuse, when requested, to take an active part in the devotional exercises.

"Soon after we removed to our station, Catharine became a member of our family, and of the school. All her energies were now bent towards the improvement of her mind, with a view to future usefulness among her people. Both in school, and in the family, her deportment was such as greatly to endear her to our hearts, and she was most tenderly loved by all the children.

"She was not *entirely* free from the inadvertences of youth; but always received reproof with great meekness, and it never failed to produce the most salutary effect.

"She was deeply sensible of the many favours she had received from Christian friends, and often, in the strongest terms expressed her gratitude.

"She was zealous in the cause of Christ, and laboured much to instruct her ignorant people in the things, that concern their everlasting peace. The advancement of the Redeemer's kingdom was to her a subject of deep interest, and she read accounts of the triumphs of the cross in heathen countries, with peculiar delight. Not many months after we settled here, a plan was devised to form a female charitable society. This plan was proposed to Catharine. She was much pleased with it, and spared no pains to explain it to the understandings of her Cherokee friends. And so successful were her exertions, that, at the meeting for the formation of the Society, at which a considerable number were present, not one refused to become a member. For the prosperity of this Society she manifested the most tender concern till her death; and she had determined, if her life should be spared to reach the Arkansas country, to use her exertions to form a similar Society there."[9]

The extracts from the diary will now be resumed, and will be continued without interruption.

EXTRACTS FROM HER DIARY.

"*Creek-Path May* 1, 1821. Commenced boarding with Mr. and Mrs. Potter. My parents live two miles from this place. I think I shall visit them almost every week, and they will come to see me often.

"2. I love to live here much. It is retired, and a good place for study. Every think looks pleasant around the school-house. The trees are covered with green leaves, and the birds sing very sweetly. How pleasant it is to be in the woods, and hear the birds praising the Lord. They remind me of the divine command, 'Remember thy Creator.' O may I never be so stupid and senseless [as to forget my Creator,] but may I remember to love and serve him, the few days I live in this world; for the time will soon come, when I must appear before him. Help me, Lord, to live to thy glory, even unto the end of my life.

"I think I feel more anxious to learn, and to understand the Bible perfectly, than I ever did before. Although I am so

---

[9] This Society first sent its annual collections to the mission at Dwight, in the Arkansas. But the last year their collection was devoted to the spread of the Gospel among the Osages. The Cherokee woman, who proposed the resolution to appropriate the money in this way, observed to the Society, "The Bible tells us to do good to our enemies, and I believe the Osages are the greatest enemies the Cherokees have." The sum was about ten dollars.

ignorant, the Saviour is able to prepare me for the usefulness among my people

"5. Saturday evening. Again I am brought to the close of another week. How have I spent my time the past week? Have I done any thing for God, and any good to my fellow creatures? I fear I have done nothing to glorify his holy name. Oh, how prone I am to sin, and to grieve the Spirit of a holy God, who is so kind in giving me time to prepare for heaven. May I improve these precious moments to the glory of my God.

"6. Sabbath evening. How thankful I ought to be to God, that he has permitted me once more to commemorate the love of a Saviour, who has shed his precious blood for the remission of sin. It was indeed a solemn season to me, and I hope refreshing to each of our souls. While sitting at the table, I thought of many sins, which I had committed against God, through my life, and how much I deserved to be case out from his presence forever. But the Son of God, who was pleased to come down from the bosom of his Father, to die on the cross for sinners like me, will, I hope, save me from death, and at last raise me to mansions of eternal rest, where I shall sit down with my blessed Jesus.

"8. This evening I have nothing to complain of, but my unfaithfulness both to God and my own soul. Have not improved my precious moments as I ought. Have learned but little in school, though my privileges are greater than those of many others. While they are ignorant of God, and have no opportunity to hear or learn about him, I am permitted to live with the children of God, where I am instructed to read the Bible, and to understand the character of Jesus. O may I be enabled to follow the example of my teachers, to live near the Saviour, and to do much good. I wish very much to be a missionary among my people. If I had an education—but perhaps I ought not to think of it. I am not worthy to be a missionary.

"14. Mr. Hoyt called on us this week, on his return from Mayhew. He gives us much interesting intelligence respecting the Choctaw mission. Mr. Hoyt expected to have brought Dr. Worcester with him, but he was too sick to travel, and was obliged to stay behind. He hopes to be able to come on soon. I long to see him. He has done a great deal towards spreading the Gospel, not only in this nation, but in other heathen nations of the earth. May the Lord restore his health, that he may see some fruits among the heathen, for whom he has been so long laboring.

"29. This day I spent my time very pleasantly at home with my dear friends. Find that brother John is the same humble believer in Jesus, walking in the Christian path. I am truly happy to meet my dear parents and sisters in health, and rejoicing in the hope of eternal glory. O may God ever delight to bless them, and to pour his Spirit richly into their hearts. I am much pleased to see them making preparations for the Sabbath. They have been engaged to-day in preparing such food, &c. as they thought would be wanting to-morrow. I think brother John and sister Susannah have done much good here with respect to the Sabbath.

"30. This day attended another solemn meeting in the house of God. Mr. Potter preached by an interpreter. I think more people than usual attended. All seemed attentive to hear the word of God. Mr. P. spoke of the importance of keeping the Sabbath holy. I hope it will not be in vain to all those who were present.

June 4. This day being *the first Monday in the month*, the people met to pray and receive religious instruction. It was truly an interesting time. The congregation, though small, was serious. One man and his wife, who have been for some time in an anxious state of mind remained after the meeting, and Mr. and Mrs. P. earnestly entreated them to seek the Lord while he was near unto them. They appeared very solemn, and said they wished to know more about God, that they might serve him the rest of their days. We hope and pray, that they may be truly converted, and become our dear brother and sister in the Lord.

"July 1. This day I have enjoyed much. Was permitted once more to sit down at the table of the Lord, and commemorate his dying love. O how good is the Saviour in permitting me to partake of his grace. May I improve my great privileges in the manner I shall wish I had done, when I come to leave the world.—P. M. Went to Mr. G.'s, where Mr. Potter preaches once in two weeks. Most of the people present were whites, from the other side of the river. It was pleasant to hear a sermon preached without an interpreter.

"Sept. 2. Think I have had a good time to-day, in praying to my heavenly father. I see nothing to trouble me, but my own wicked heart. It appears to me, that the more I wish to serve God, the more I sin. I seem never to have done any thing good in the sight of God. But the time is short, when I shall be delivered from this body of sin, and enter the kingdom of heaven.

"3. The first Monday in the month. No doubt many Christians have been this day praying for my poor nation, as well as for other heathen nations or the earth. O why do I live so little concerned for my own soul, and for the souls of others? Why is it that I pray no more to God? Is it because he is not merciful? Oh no. He is good, kind, merciful? Oh no. He is good, kind, merciful, always ready to answer the prayers of his children. O for more love to my Savior than I now have.

"4. I am now with my sister, with whom I expect to spend a few days. I hope the Lord will make our communion sweet.

"Visited at Mr. —'s, but had no opportunity of conversing with Mrs. — on religious subjects, as we intended to have done. Mr. — said he had seen so many different ways among professed Christians, that it was hard to tell who was right. I felt too ignorant to instruct such a well educated man; though I knew, that there is *but one* way under heaven, whereby men can be saved, and that is, by coming to Him, who came to seek and to save that which was lost.

"9. Returned yesterday from sister G's. Found the mission family in good health. I cannot express how much I love the missionaries, with whom I live. I do not feel my privileges, until I am away from them, and mingle with worldly people. Then I long to get back to be with Christians.

"I rejoice and bless my heavenly Father, that he has kept my dear brother John, and permitted me to meet him once more in the land of the living. I am sorry to see him so unwell, and fear he will not recover. But the Lord's will be done, and not mine. I know that he will do all things for the good of those who love him.

"Left home, in company with brother John and sister Susannah, [his wife,] for the purpose of visiting the Sulphur Springs in Blount county, Alabama.

"21. About noon we came to a spring, which is said to possess the same qualities with those we intended to visit, and we concluded to make it the place of our abode for a few days. We therefore pitched our tent a few yards from the water, and at night spread our blankets on the ground, and slept very well.

"22. Feel very uneasy respecting my brother, he is so unwell. May the Lord be with us in this lonely place.

"23. Brother John drinks the water, and bathes in it, but has yet received no benefit. I do not feel so well as I did before I came here, and almost wish to return immediately. Perhaps it is lying on the ground, that makes me feel sick. But if brother John had a comfortable place to sleep, I should not care for myself. The Lord knows what is best for us.

"24. We expect a boy with our horses to-day, and hope to reach home tomorrow. Saw Mr. J. R. to-day in a very low state of health. Conversed with him a little on the subject of religion. This I really felt was my duty, as I thought it likely I should never have another opportunity. He said, he was very wicked, and afraid to die. I told him we were all wicked, but the Saviour, who was willing to die for us, would pardon our sins, if we would only give ourselves to him. He replied, that when he was in health, he did not do his duty towards God, but if he recovered he would try to do better. As he was not able to converse much, I commended him to God, and left him. God is able to make him his dear child, and to prepare him for heaven.

"Jan. 3, 1822. This was truly a solemn and interesting day to me, one which will never be forgotten. My dear father and mother were baptized in the name of the Holy Trinity. How kind is our Creator, in his willingness to take notice of us sinful worms of the dust, and allowing us to become acquainted with Jesus Christ. O may we walk close with God, and be enabled to set such an example to others, that they may be led to glorify our Father, who is in heaven.

"14. Have not attended school since last vacation, having been at home taking care of my sick brother. He has failed very fast, the past week. I fear he will not live many days. The will of the Lord be done.

"16. My dear brother is very low. Perhaps he will soon depart from this sinful world, and fly to the arms of his blessed Redeemer. Had some conversation with him in the evening. His mind seemed to be in a happy state. He asked me, whether, after his decease, I thought we should stay here, or go to the Arkansas. I told him I hoped he would be restored to health. He said he thought that was very doubtful, and added, that he thought brother Webber would come for us after his departure. My heart was full. I could make no reply.

"18. Mr. Butrick and John Arch, who have been visiting us for a few days past, left us this morning, with the intention of going through the nation, preaching Jesus Christ to those, who are in darkness. This will probably take three months. May the Lord go with his dear servants on their long journey through the wilderness, and bless their labours to many immortal souls. I cannot sufficiently express my gratitude to God, for sending out missionaries to this distant land, that we, who were wanderers in the wild woods, might find the road to heaven. How kindly are they inviting us to come and partake of the rich feast, which has been provided for all who will accept it. Yet how few are willing to comply with the invitation! Frequently do I weep for my Cherokee brothers and sisters, when I consider their awful situations while out of Christ; and willingly would I offer myself for their assistance, were I qualified for a religious teacher. I hope God will prepare me to do some good among the heathen. O that it may be my greatest desire to do the will of my heavenly Father. I am determined to pray for my people, while God lends me breath; and when I die, may my Saviour receive me to my heavenly home, to join with millions of saints in singing the praises of redeeming love through a never-ending eternity.

"29. Eternity seems near. A few days more, and if I am indeed a child of God, I shall walk the golden streets of the New Jerusalem. O happy day, when I shall see all the Christians, who have ever lived, and when God himself shall be my joy.

"30. Brother John is senseless most of the time. I fear he is to remain but a little while in this world. But in that case he will soon go to his Father in heaven. May we be submissive, knowing that he, who sent us into this world, has a right to call us hence whenever he sees best. Our great consolation is, that our dear brother will soon be freed from pain, and rest in the bosom of his dear Jesus.

"31. Had the pleasure of seeing Mr. and Mrs. Potter at this place. I love them, as *my own* brother and sister.

"Feb. 2. My dear brother very sick. O thou blessed Jesus, take him not away by this sickness. Restore him to health, that he may live long, and be a great blessing to our nation But O may I be submissive to thy holy will.

"Sabbath morning. Painful is it to record, that my dear brother John appears, this day, to be on the borders of eternity ! Lord, come near to us at this time. Help us to give up our dear brother into thy hands.

"Evening. Brother John is no more ! O distressing thought, he has gone to return no more! But we shall soon go to him. I trust, indeed, we have much reason to believe he has gone to Christ his Saviour. Through his sickness he seemed reconciled to the will of God, and said he was not afraid to die. He said, that though his sufferings were great, they were nothing in comparison with Christ's sufferings. About a week before he died, he spoke to the family as follows:—"It is now more than a year since we began to follow Christ, and what have we done for him? Do we live like Christians? I fear we do not. I do not hear you talk to the people about our Saviour, when they come to visit you. We are professors of religion, and why is it that we do not show it to others? You should always remember to keep the Sabbath holy. You are too much occupied in domestic concerns on the Sabbath, so that you cannot get time to converse about God.' He asked me, if the missionaries did their cooking on the Sabbath. I told him, their preparations were made before the Sabbath. He said, 'that is what we ought to do.' He frequently requested me to read and explain the Bible to him, which was my great delight."

Here ends her diary. And the reader will doubtless wish that all had been saved, breathing, as it does, so much good sense and unfeigned piety.

Of her brother John, the journal of the mission at Brainerd contains the following eulogium, penned on hearing of his death.

"Two years ago he was in heathenish darkness. About that time, his brother and sister told him of the Bible, and some of the important truths it contained; and he soon felt an unconquerable desire to read it. He could then talk and understand familiar English. Soon after, a school was opened in his neighbourhood, and he applied himself, with the most unwearied diligence, to study. In the course of six months, he learned to read intelligibly; read the New Testament through once, and about half through again; wrote a number of legible letters to his friends; became a hopeful convert to the Christian religion, and a member of the Church of Christ, which he continued to adorn by an exemplary life, till his departure from these dark and afflictive scenes, to join, as we trust, the Church of the first-born in heaven."

Soon after the decease of this brother, Catharine accompanied her father to Huntsville, in the state of Alabama.

Here, either at that time, or later in the season, she spent two or three months, in the family of Dr. Alexander A. Campbell, a pious and esteemed physician. Dr. Campbell had seen her at her father's house before she went to Brainerd, and was so favourably impressed, by her personal appearance, that he subsequently procured for her a Bible, and some other religious books, which were forwarded, but never received.

Nearly five years had elapsed since that interview. Dr. Campbell's own words, extracted from his letter to the Rev. Mr. Potter of Creek-Path, shall describe the impression, which she now made upon him, and upon others in Huntsville.

"She was not now the wild, untutored girl she was then. She was graceful and polite, and humility and benevolence beamed from her countenance. Some of my acquaintance were unwilling to believe she was an Indian.

"At your request, I returned with her to her nation to see a diseased Indian child, and though it was at the expense of neglecting important professional business, I was amply repaid, by the interesting conversation I had with her, on literary and religious subjects.

"At first, she was backward to enter into free conversation. A diffident reserve was a prominent trait in her character. But when we became well acquainted, I found her perfectly agreeable and intelligent on any ordinary subject. But her favourite theme was the SAVIOR. She dwelt much, also, on the situation of her people, and manifested the greatest solicitude for their spiritual interests; often expressing the hope, that I would come and live among them, and teach them respecting the Lord Jesus.

"During the summer of this year, she spent several months in my family. A part of that time she was suffering very severely from a bilious fever, which she bore with all possible patience and resignation, never showing that peevishness and fretfulness so common in persons recovering from that disease. She always looked upon her afflictions as resulting from the chastising hand of God, and designed for her improvement.

"She received very marked attentions from the visitors at my house, and many of the principal families in the town sought an acquaintance with her, appeared sensible of her worth, and esteemed her friendship highly. These attentions, so far from exciting her vanity, had the effect to humble her the more. She appeared ever to think much less highly of herself, than others thought of her. I have often been astonished to see how the flattering addresses and high encomiums of people of elevated standing in society, seemed to render her more distrustful of her own worth."

This, though evidently the warm language of friendship, is justified by the concurrent testimony of all the intimate friends of Catharine.

In September 1822, at the earnest request of her parents, she left the family of Mr. Potter to reside with them. Being engaged, at that time, in some favourite studies, it was a great trial to leave the school. But so tender was her regard for her aged parents, that she made not the least objection.

Near the close of the year 1822, the Rev. Reynolds Bascom, accompanied by several Indian youth from the Foreign Mission School at Cornwall, arrived at Creek-Path, on his way to Elliot, where he designed to spend a few months in missionary labour.

"Here," says Mr. Bascom, "I had an opportunity of seeing the precious fruits of missionary instruction and divine grace, in the intelligence, amiable manners, and Christian temper, of Catharine, and other members of the little church which had been formed in the place, chiefly among her family connexions.

"The impression made on my mind by my first interview, which was at her father's house, was that of uncommon simplicity, modesty and meekness. We arrived after the family had dined, and she received us and spread a table for our refreshment, with the unaffected kindness of a sister. The gracefulness of her figure, and the sweetness of her expression, have often been the subject of remark; and I was the more delighted with her humility, as I greatly feared I should discover an unhappy influence from the misjudged praise, which had been heaped upon her. The fact was, she gave me evidence, by her habitual behavior, of being a sanctified child of God."

It was soon after her removal to her paternal home, that the disease, the seeds of which had, probably for several years, been germinating in her constitution, began to assume an aspect, which excited some alarm.

In consequence of this, she took a journey to Brainerd, in February 1823, with the view of consulting Dr. Butler, a medical gentleman residing at that station. She hoped, also, to derive benefits from the journey. These hopes were disappointed. A cold, tempestuous storm arose, soon after she left home, to the whole of which she was unavoidably exposed; and the slight cough, to which she had, for some time, been subject, was very much increased. She spent three weeks at Brainerd, and then returned to Creek-Path, intending to obtain permission from her parents to place herself again under the care of Dr. Butler. But her increased illness rendered her unable to encounter the fatigues of another journey.

The narrative must now be interrupted, in order that several letters, written during the time embraced by this chapter, may be introduced. A part of the first, and the fourth, were published in the narrative of the "Little Osage Captive." The third made its first appearance in the New Haven Religious Intelligencer.

TO HER BROTHER DAVID, AT CORNWALL.

Creek-Path, Aug. 12, 1820.

My dear Brother,

Your dear lines I received this evening, for which I thank you. I hope they will not be the last you will write me. O dear brother, how much it would rejoice my heart to see you this evening, and converse with you face to face! But our good Lord has separated us, perhaps never to see each other again in this world. I often think of the morning you left Brainerd. It was a solemn hour, and I trust it was a sweet season to our souls. We wept, and prayed, and sung together before our dear Saviour; and longed for that blessed day, when we should meet, to part no more. What is a short separation in this world? Nothing compared to an eternal separation! How thankful we ought to be then, my dear brother, that we have a hope to be saved through the blessed Lamb of God. Yes, I trust when our bodies shall die, our souls shall be raised above the sky, where we shall dwell together, in singing the praises of Him who bought us with his precious blood. I hope we shall meet our parents, and brothers, and sisters there. Since you left, the Lord has reached down his arm, to take sinners from darkness, into the marvellous light of the Gospel. Dear brother, let us praise and rejoice continually in the Lord, for his goodness to our dear people, in giving them hearts to love and praise his holy name. Surely the Lord is with us here. We feel his presence. Our dear father and mother are inquiring what they shall do to be saved. Mother says she is grieved to think her children are going to leave her behind. But she says she will pray as long as she lives, and that the Saviour will pardon her sins, that she may go with her children to heaven.

I hope you will write to our parents as often as you can. I sometimes think the Saviour has given them new hearts, especially our dear father. He appears quite changed.

Soon after you left Brainerd, I was called here to take charge of a school of females, about two miles from home. I take great delight in teaching. The number of girls in school is twenty-eight. They are very good children, and learn fast. Sister Anna is assisting me in the school. She rejoices with us to hear from you in this distant land.

O dear brother, I hope you will pray for me. Pray that I may do good to the immortal souls of my pupils. Sometimes the work appears too great for me, and I am almost discouraged. But I know, He that has called me to work in his vineyard, is able to keep me.

I could tell you a great many good things, if I had time. But I must stop, after asking your prayers for all your Creek-Path friends. I hope when you return to your nation, you will find many Christians. Farewell, dear brother; may the Lord be with you, and prepare you for great usefulness in the world. This is the prayer of your sister

CATHARINE BROWN.

TO MR. AND MRS. HALL.

Creek-Path, Nov. 19, 1820.

My dear Brother and Sister,

THIS is the first opportunity I have had to answer the kind letter, which you wrote some time since. I thank you for it, and hope you will forgive me for not writing sooner. I think of you every day, and long to see you once more in this world. I often think of the happy hours we used to spend together, while I was with you at Brainerd. But the happy hours are gone, I fear never to return. I hope, if we may not meet in this world, we may in heaven, where we shall never be separated. O, my dear friends, do you not sometimes long to see that glorious day, when Christians shall be gathered from all parts of the world to sing the praises of our dear Redeemer? What a day it will be for Christians! And shall we be among the number? Sometimes I fear I shall not be, my wicked heart is so prone to sin. But I know the blood of Christ is sufficient to wash away all my sins, and prepare me for his eternal glory. I will, therefore, commit myself to God. It is all that I can do.

O how good it is to lie at the feet of Jesus, and feel ourselves purified by his blood. Then we have no reason to fear what the world can do unto us.

My dear friends, I cannot tell you how much I love you, because you were willing to leave your native land, and your dear people, to come into this heathen part of the world, to instruct me and my people in the way of salvation. May the Lord reward you for this labour of love. Probably you must have some trials to pass through, as other missionaries do; but we ought to rejoice, that we are accounted worthy to labour for

CATHARINE BROWN

God. Our days will soon be past, and if we are the children of God, we shall soon be at rest in the bosom of our dear Saviour.

My father, mother, brothers, and sisters, wish to be remembered affectionately to you. Write often. I am always happy to hear from you.

From your sister,
CATHARINE BROWN.

TO HER BROTHER DAVID.

Creek-Path, Feb. 21, 1821.

My dear Brother,

I RECEIVED your kind letter some time since, and it gave me great satisfaction to hear from you. I should have written to you before this time, but did not know how to send to Brainerd. I am truly happy to hear that you feel so well contented with your situation in school, and that you are well pleased with your dear instructor. Our dear parents are in good health. They have removed from the place where they lived before, and are now living with brother John. I think they have truly passed from death unto life. They seem to be growing in grace and in the knowledge of Him who has redeemed their souls from hell. Indeed, you cannot imagine how different they seem from what they did when you left us. All they desire now, is to do the will of our dear Saviour. This work is the Lord's, and no doubt he will keep them and carry them safe through this sinful world, until he receives them to his heavenly kingdom. O, dear brother, truly the Lord has heard our prayers for the souls of our parents. We have great reason to rejoice. May we not say,—not unto us, but to thy name be all the praise? You have doubtless heard that brother John has joined the church. Dear brother David, my heart is full while I am writing. How shall I express my gratitude to God for bringing him to a knowledge of the Saviour.

He says sometimes he feels happy in praying to God, and feels willing that he should do with him as seemeth good in his sight.

My brother David, when we look back and see what the Lord has done for our family in the course of a few years, O let us call upon our souls, and all that is within us, to praise our God for his great blessings to us.

I sometimes long to see your face once more in this world, to converse and pray with you before our Saviour. I often think of the happy hours, which we spent when we were at Brainerd, when we first tasted the sweetness of religion, and when we used to take each other's hand to walk and sing our favourite hymn,

"Come we that love the Lord."

We then knew the happiness of saints, and felt that religion was not 'designed to make our pleasures less.' But now our heavenly Father has separated us for a time in this world; I hope for his glory, and for the good of perishing souls around us. We have much to do for our Saviour. As we hope we are children of the most high God, let us be good soldiers, and not be weary in well-going, for in due season we shall reap if we faint not.

Father and mother send love to you, and to the scholars in Cornwall. I hope you will write to us soon, and let us know how you do.

Adieu, dear brother, till we meet again,

CATHARINE BROWN.

TO THE SAME.

Creek-Path, 1821.

My dear Brother,

ALTHOUGH we may be separated many hundreds of miles, the God of the Universe, whom we serve, will often give us the enjoyment of himself, which you know is of far greater value than all this world can afford. Last Sabbath was a very solemn and interesting day to us. Rev. Mr. W. from the state of New York was here—a very pious and engaged Christian. We were much refreshed by his kind instructions. I think it was truly a pleasant day to my soul. The sacrament was administered, and we were permitted once more to sit at the table of the Lord, and commemorate his dying love. Mr. S. was baptized. Also an infant of Mrs. F. named Samuel Worcester. The congregation were attentive and some of them were affected to tears. I hope the time is not far distant, when all the heathen shall be brought to the knowledge of the Redeemer. We have recently formed a Female Society[10] in this place. The members pay fifty cents a year. I trust you will pray that we may be blessed, and that we may be instrumental in the great work of building up the cause of the Redeemer. I can never be sufficiently thankful to God for sending us missionaries, to teach us the way we should go. We love them as our own brothers and sisters. That you may enjoy the light of our Saviour's countenance, while in this short journey of life, and finally be received to mansions of eternal glory, is the prayer of your sister,

CATHARINE BROWN.

TO MR. AND MRS. HALL.

Creek-Path, June 1,1822.

My dear Brother and Sister Hall,

SWEET and reviving is the thought, that we are not to continue long in this world, but hope soon to rest in the city of our God. My dear brother and sister, be patient in all your trials and hardships, remembering that you are laboring for God, and not for man alone. The Saviour will give you an unfading crown of glory in due season. I often think of the glorious day, when I shall meet you, and all good missionaries, in the kingdom of our Saviour. I shall then be always with those dear friends, who have told me so much about heaven, and taught me to love and

---

[10] The Society, of which mention was made at p. 41.

serve Christ. I hope you will not forget to pray, that I may possess more of the spirit of Christ.

The pupils in the school here generally make good improvement. The religious prospects are encouraging. Meetings on the Sabbath, and weekly conferences, are well attended. The church appears well. Last Sabbath I, for the first time, met my parents at the table of the Lord.

I have many things to tell you; but my health will not allow me to write much at one time. The little I have written gives me pain. My health has been feeble for some weeks past, but my complaints are not alarming. I shall try to visit you next vacation, if life is spared. Will my dear brother and sister write soon to the affectionate CATHARINE.

TO HER BROTHER DAVID.

Huntsville, Aug. 30, 1822.

My dear Brother,

I AM sorry to tell you, that I have but a few moments of time to write this evening. I came here the 13th inst. and expect to return in a few weeks.

I left our friends all very well, and walking in the fear of God. I should have written long before this, had I not been sick; but my health is now much better than it was when I left home. Brother David, remember that your sister Catharine loves you much, and prays for you every day. I trust you will not return before you are prepared to preach the Gospel. Let me know your feelings in this respect when you write again, and I shall know how to pray for you. I do not expect you to go through all the studies, that ministers generally do in New England, but wish you to be qualified enough to withstand the enemies of God, and teach the truths of Christianity. If your health does not permit you to study, and your hesitation of speech still continues, I should not think it was your duty to pursue your studies.

However, I know the Lord will make every path of duty plain before you. Do not think we are unhappy. It is true we were greatly tried, last winter, in losing our dear brother. But, blessed be God, it was not more than we are able to bear.

We feel it was good for us to be afflicted, knowing that the Lord is good, and will always do what is right. I have not time to write all I wish to send you. When I return home, you shall have a long letter from your affectionate sister

CATHARINE.

TO THE SAME, AT ANDOVER.

Creek-Path, Jan. 18, 1823.

My dear Brother,

YOURS of Nov. 2, 1822, was received a few days since. I am much gratified to hear, that you are to continue in New England another year. I hope you will be the better qualified for usefulness to our countrymen, when you return. I pray for you daily, that God may be with you and bless you in your undertaking.

I feel anxious to see you, yet I am willing to have you stay until you have received further education. How has your mind been exercised since you entered the interesting Seminary at Andover? Are you living in the enjoyment of the religion of Christ? We must, dear brother, live near to God, and be engaged in his cause, if we would be his followers. Let us, then, not calculate to live in idleness and ease, unconcerned for the salvation of souls.

We are under great obligations to honour God before the world, and to be active in his service. Let us not hide our talents in the earth, for the Lord will require them of us. There is a crown of glory laid up for those who are faithful unto the end.

It is now eleven months, since our dear brother John departed from this lower world, and entered the unseen regions of eternity, where I hope he is now walking in the streets of the New Jerusalem, filled with holy love. Oh boundless love, and matchless grace, of our Lord and Saviour Jesus Christ! How happy shall we feel when we land on the shores of eternal felicity. There we shall meet our dear brother, and all who have gone before us, and shall reign in the paradise of God forever and ever.

I often think of our relations in the Arkansas. I long to hear of their conversion. Let us not neglect to pray for them daily; particularly for brother W. The Lord, I hope, will renew his heart, and make him abundantly useful to the cause of missions.

We rejoice to see brother A. once more in our dwellings. After a long journey from the Arkansas country, he arrived here, much fatigued, in the latter part of November. He intends to spend a few months with us, and then return with sister Susan. I do not feel very well about her going into the wilderness, and far from Christian society, where she will perhaps have no religious instruction.

Her mother has removed thirty or forty miles from the missionary station [at Dwight.] But we commend her into the hands of the Almighty, who is able to keep her from evil, and from all the temptations of this delusive world. I am glad to hear from our relations in that country. Brother Walter was expecting to set out in a few days for the city of Washington, and had thoughts of visiting some of the northern States before he returned. It is likely you may see him in New England. He has placed brother Edmund in the missionary school at Dwight, to continue three or four years. He has become very steady and attentive to his books. I hope the Lord will give him a new heart, and prepare him for usefulness.

Brother W. has given up trading, and has commenced farming. He has purchased land in the Osage country, at the Salt Springs. Whether he intends removing his family to that place, I know not. It is my prayer, that he may be brought to bow to the scepter of King Jesus, in whom is life everlasting. As for our going to the Arkansas, it is not decided. Perhaps we shall know better, when you return. You know mother is always very anxious to remove to that country, but father is not. For my own part, I feel willing to do whatever is duty, and the will of our parents. I feel willing to go, or stay. The Lord will direct all things right, and in him may we put all our trust.

We had the pleasure of seeing your schoolmates McKee and Israel Folsom. They called on us on their way to the Choctaw nation. They said there were many good people at the north. They had rather live among the Yankees, than any other people. I hope they will be very useful to their nation.

Mr. Potter has gone to Brainerd on some business, and I shall stay with Mrs. P. until he returns. We expect him home this week. I hope he will bring a large packet of letters from our Brainerd friends. Mrs. P. is engaged in teaching school while her husband is absent. Several of the scholars are very attentive, and make good progress in their studies. Sarah is in the first class. She is a good girl to learn, and is much beloved by her teacher. She has begun to read the Bible in course, and has read partly through the Memoirs of Miss Caroline Smelt. When I wrote to you last, I was in a declining state of health, and for that reason I left my studies to have more exercise. The Lord has been pleased to restore me to my usual health, and I now feel pretty well.

I spent two months in Huntsville, last spring, in the family of Dr. Campbell. Mrs.— is a very pious and engaged Christian. I became acquainted with several pious families in Huntsville, who, I believe, feel interested in the cause of missions. The pious ladies made up clothing for the children in Creek-Path. We hope this is only the beginning of a missionary spirit in that place.

I am glad to tell you, that our female Society is growing in its numbers. We have collected nearly double the sum this year that we did last. The Society has concluded to send our money for this year to the Arkansas mission.

I am glad the people are so willing to assist in advancing the Redeemer's kingdom in our heathen land. May the glorious period soon arrive, when all the nations of the earth shall be brought to the knowledge of the truth as it is in Jesus. Oh, dear brother, though we are widely separated in person, yet we are near in spirit, and can unite our prayers for the approach of this happy day.

O let us do with our might what our hands find to do. I am now in my little study. I have spent in this room many happy hours in prayer to my Heavenly Father. But Oh, how cold and stupid my heart is! How little I feel for the salvation of souls!

> Oh, for a closer walk with God,
> A calm and heavenly frame;
> And light to shine upon the road,
> That leads me to the Lamb.

Please to write soon, and tell me every thing respecting your present situation.

CATHARINE BROWN.

TO THE SAME.

Brainerd, Feb. 10, 1823.

My dear brother David,

I AM at Brainerd, on a visit from Creek-Path. My heart is filled with gratitude to God, in being permitted to see these dear missionaries once more, and unite with them in praise to our Lord and Saviour. I feel truly attached to Brainerd, where I first found the Saviour; and O how I love the dear sisters, with whom I have spent many happy hours, both in school, and in walking to the house of worship. But those happy hours are past. We must be contented, and look forward to that day when we shall meet to part no more.

I left home last week, in company with Mr. Boudinot, and sister Susan. Hope my journey will be beneficial to my health.

If our dear father and mother are willing, I intend to pursue study again, as soon as I return home.

There is some seriousness among the people in our neighbourhood. Several are very anxious to receive religious instruction. When I return, I think I shall make it my business to go round, once in two weeks, to read and explain the Scriptures to the females.

I cannot but hope the Lord will continue to have mercy on our people, and will bring many to the knowledge of the truth as it is in Jesus.

I hope you will write to our dear parents soon. They are always happy to hear from you.

From your affectionate sister

CATHARINE BROWN.

CHAPTER V.

HER SICKNESS AND DEATH.

Brief agitations of her mind.—Her love for her people.—Is visited by Dr. Campbell.—Letter to Mrs. Campbell.—Alarming symptom in her disease.—Her resignation and consolations.—Dr. Campbell advises her removal to Limestone.—State of her mind at this time.—Strong manifestations of affection for her at Creek-Path.—Account of her removal.—Temporary improvement in her health.—Dictates a letter to her brother David.—Hopes of her recovery relinquished.—This fact stated to her father and herself.—Her last hours, death, and burial.—Monument over her grave.

THE attention of the reader is now invited to the closing scenes in the life of Catharine, where her faith in her Saviour will be seen to have been signally triumphant over the terrors of the grave.

After she returned from Brainerd, she seems generally to have considered her removal from the world as not very distant, and to have spent much time in reflecting on death and its consequences. These subjects she not unfrequently made the topics of conversation. One instance of this kind is described by Mrs. Potter.

"Entering her room, one evening, at an early hour, I found she had retired with unusual debility. She requested me to read, from some medical author, the symptoms of consumption. I complied; and, after comparing them with her own, she expressed a belief, that she had that disease. I inquired what were her feelings in view of this conclusion. She replied, with tears, 'I am not prepared to die.' You have a hope, I said, of happiness beyond the grave? 'Yes, I have a hope resting on the promises of the Saviour; but I have been unfaithful!'

"We were both too much affected to say more, and remained for some time silent. At length Catharine sweetly raised her voice and said, 'Sister Potter how beautiful is this hymn;' and then she repeated

> 'Why should we start and fear to die!
>   What timorous worms we mortals are!
> Death is the gate of endless joy,
>   And yet we dread to enter there.
>
> 'The pains, and groans, and dying strife
>   Fright our approaching souls away;
> Still we shrink back again to life,
>   Fond of our prison and our clay.
>
> 'Oh, if my Lord would come and meet,
>   My soul should stretch her wings in haste;
> Fly fearless through death's iron gate,
>   Nor feel the terrors as she passed.
>
> 'Jesus can make a dying bed
>   Feel soft as downy pillows are,
> While on his breast I lean my head,
>   And breathe my life out sweetly there.'

"I inquired if she could adopt this as the language of her heart, and she answered with great meekness, that she hoped she could."

It does not appear, that, after this, her mind was again seriously disturbed by apprehensions respecting *her own* future well-being.

But when she saw her aged parents in an infirm state of health, and needing all the attentions of an affectionate daughter, and when, moreover, she reflected how many of her dear people remained ignorant of the only Saviour of sinners, she clung to life, and her earnest prayer was, that she might recover. We are informed, that her trials from these sources were, at one time, very severe.

She said to a beloved friend, "I know, that it is my duty to submit entirely to the will of God. He can carry on his work without me. He can take care of my parents. Yet I am anxious to recover. I wish to labour more for my people."

How strong her desires were for the improvement of her people, is further evident from this fact, that though David was the only surviving brother, who had the same mother with herself, and though he was dearer to her than any one else, except her parents, she was, for some time, unwilling he should be informed of her sickness, lest he should be induced to leave his studies, and come home to see her. Much as she loved him, she said she had rather he would remain in New England, until he was prepared to preach Christ to his countrymen.

In April she was visited by that kind friend of herself and family, Dr. Campbell. He strongly advised, that she should remove to his house, thinking it probable that he might then relieve her. Her friends all consented, only desiring her to remain at home a few days, till the departure of her brother Webber, who had come from the Arkansas. But his stay was unexpectedly prolonged a month. During this time, Catharine failed so rapidly, that she was unable to ride to Limestone, where Dr. Campbell then resided.

On this occasion, Catharine thus wrote to Mrs. Campbell.

Creek-Path, April 17, 1823.

My dear Mrs. Campbell,

MY heart was made truly glad this morning, by the arrival of Dr. Campbell. I have long been very anxious to see him, on account of the low state of my health. For two months past, it has been declining, and I am now reduced to extreme debility.

This affliction I view as coming from my heavenly Father. I deserve correction, and hope to bear the chastising rod with humble submission.

I have a wish to recover, that I may be useful to my poor countrymen, but know, that all human means will be ineffectual without the blessing of God. I pray that Dr. Campbell may be the instrument in his hands of restoring me to health. If the weather were pleasant, I should be disposed to return with him.

I thank you for your present, and wish I had something valuable to send in return. Dr. Campbell will hand you a little ribbond. When you wear it, remember Catharine.

Mrs. P. sends love, and hopes to receive a visit from you ere long. Much love to the children.

Farewell, my friend, my sister. May heaven grant you its choicest blessings, and reward you an hundred fold for all your kindness to me. Again I say, farewell. May we meet in heaven. Yours affectionately.

CATHARINE BROWN.

As she approached nearer to eternity, her faith evidently grew stronger, and she became more and more able cheerfully to resign, not only to herself, but her parents, her friends, her people, her all, to the disposal of her Lord.

May 15th she was reduced very low by a hemorrhage from the lungs, and for a few days was viewed as upon the borders of the grave.

Before this alarming symptom, it had been proposed to send again for Dr. Campbell. But her parents were persuaded first to try the skill of some Indian practitioners. Their prescriptions were followed, until the hemorrhage occurred. Then her alarmed parents sent immediately for Mr. Potter, hoping he could do something to relieve their darling child. Providentially the Rev. Reynolds Bascom, of whom mention has been already made, had just arrived from the Choctaw nation, on his way to the northern States; and having been afflicted in a similar manner himself, he was able to administer effectual remedies.

It is pleasing to be able to insert here the notices, which Mr. Bascom made, at the time, respecting his interview with her, in this hour of trial.

"May 15. Rode to brother Potter's, before breakfast. Soon after our arrival, a message came, that Catharine Brown had been taken with bleeding at the lungs, and brother Potter was requested to visit her. We accordingly rode over to her father's house immediately after breakfast, and found her entirely prostrated by a copious hemorrhage. After bleeding her in the arm, she experienced a sensible relief.

"16. Visited Catharine, with brother Potter, and found it necessary to bleed her again. Conversed and prayed with her, and left her in a peaceful frame of mind.

"19. Left Creek-Path for Brainerd. Brother Potter rode with us to Mr. Brown's. Catharine appeared sweetly composed. Her countenance was cheerful, and her soul filled with tenderness and filial trust in God. After conversation and prayer, I asked her what she would have me say to her brother David.

"She replied, 'Tell him not to be uneasy about *me*. If I do not meet him in this world, I hope to meet him in heaven. I have a great desire to see him, but the Lord may not permit us to meet here.' These words were spoken in a low, but audible whisper, and with the significant emphasis of a heart filled with faith and love.

"I have rarely, if ever, seen a more lovely object for the pencil, than she appeared to me on her dying bed. The natural mildness of her features seemed lighted with a beam of heavenly hope, and her whole aspect was that of a mature Christian, waiting, with filial patience, the welcome summons to the presence of her Lord."

Mrs. Potter says,—"Death was now disarmed of his terrors. She could look into the grave without alarm. She confessed her sins with great meekness, and mourned that she had not been more faithful in the service of God; yet rejoiced to resign her soul into the hands of her Redeemer.

"Once, when I visited her, she affectionately took my hand and said,—'My dear sister, I have been wishing to see you, for several days. I have thought a great deal of you and Mr. Potter. I love you much, but am going to leave you. I think I shall not live long. You have done much for me. I thank you, and hope the Lord will reward you. I am willing to die, if it be the will of God. I know that I have experienced his love. I have no desire to live in this world, but to do good. But God can carry on his work without me. I hope you will continue the meetings of females. You must not be discouraged. I thought when I should get to the Arkansas, I would form a society among the females, like ours. But I shall never live to get there. I feel for my dear parents, but the Lord will take care of them.'

"At another interview she said,—'I feel perfectly resigned to the will of God. I know he will do right with his children. I thank God, that I am entirely in his hands. I feel willing to live, or die, as he thinks best. My only wish is, that he may be glorified. I hope, should I ever recover, I shall be more faithful in the cause of Christ, than I have ever been.' "

A request was sent to Dr. Campbell to visit her as soon as possible. But he was unable to come till the 21st, by which time Catharine was so much enfeebled, as to be entirely confined to her room. She could not even raise herself without assistance. The physician gave it as his opinion, that she could live but a few days, unless she was removed to Limestone, it being impossible for him to attend on her at so great a distance. Whether such a removal was possible, was at first doubted. But a kind Providence furnished unexpectedly such facilities for the measure, that it was determined on.

Before entering on an account of her removal, some further notices of the state of her mind will be given.

Just before her leaving home, she requested a friend to write thus, on her behalf, to her brother David. "I am entirely resigned to the will of God, and hope you will feel the same resignation. I am perfectly willing to die, or to live, as the Lord shall direct. This world is nothing but sin. I have no wish to live in it, but to do good. If it be the Lord's will to take me now, I am willing to go."

"Religious confidence and tranquility," says Dr. Campbell, "were at this time her sweet companions. How happy she seemed in my view, so near the confines of the eternal world, about to relinquish all earthly cares and sorrows for the enjoyment of her dear Redeemer's presence!

"On the 23d, she seemed to have the most cheering evidence of her interest in the Lord Jesus. Thus she exclaimed,—'Now I am ready to die. Oh, how delightful is the view of my Saviour! How happy shall I be, when I arrive at my Father's house.'

"On being asked, what would be her feelings, if it was the will of God she should live, she replied; 'The Lord's will be done, and not mine. If I can promote his cause in any way, I am desirous to live. But if I am taken away, I hope my brother David will be useful, in bringing our benighted nation to a knowledge of Jesus.'

"Her soul appeared full, and more than full, of love to God. She spoke much of his goodness to her, and expressed much regret, that she had done so little in his cause. The day preceding this, she had expressed a wish to go to Huntsville, and unite with Mrs. L. and C. in forming an association for prayer, and in endeavouring to do something for the cause of Christ."

Catharine was now unable to endure the motion of a carriage, even for a short distance. It would be necessary, therefore, in proceeding to Limestone, to carry her on a litter to the Tennessee river, which was six miles distant; then to take her in a boat down the river, forty miles, to a village named Trienna; and from thence, on a litter again, about five miles, to Dr. Campbell's. But, in order to the successful prosecution of this enterprise, the aid of some person, through the whole distance, who was acquainted with the English language, was indispensable. And it should be thankfully noted, that, just when the question of removal was agitated, Mr. William Leech, a pious acquaintance from Huntsville, providentially arrived at Creek-Path, and very kindly tendered his services.

Monday, the 26th of May, was the time appointed for commencing the journey.

"Numbers," says Mrs. Potter, "assembled to take, as they feared, and as it proved, a last look of their beloved friend. After a prayer, in which she was commended to the divine protection, the canoe was announced to be in readiness, and we followed the litter, borne by her affectionate people, to the river. Old and young were bathed in tears, and some were obliged to use their influence to prevent a general and loud lamentation. Catharine alone was calm, while she bade farewell to those she tenderly loved."

Mr. Leech says, that small groups of her acquaintance were frequently seen on the road, waiting her approach. When she arrived where they were, they would hasten to the side of the litter, take her by the hand, and often walk away without speaking a word, the tears all the while rolling down their cheeks."

Two or three extracts from Mr. Leech's narrative of the voyage and journey, from the time of her embarkation on the river, will be inserted.

"About 4 o'clock, P. M. on the 26th, we began to glide quite pleasantly down the stream, accompanied by several of Catharine's relatives. Our design was to stop as soon as it became dark, until the moon arose. But we could discover no suitable place for landing, till daylight was gone, and then the difficulty was increased. The margin of the river was generally covered with brushwood. In some places, the shore was a deep mire; at others, there were bluffs and rocks. This made landing difficult and dangerous in the dark; and along this part of the river were scarcely any settlements.

"At length the danger of running was such, as to determine us to get upon the land in some way. We accordingly steered towards the shore, and providentially discovered a good landing-place, near which was also a house, where our party was kindly entertained, and our various wants supplied. Had we passed this place, we should not have found such another, for twenty miles.

"When the moon was sufficiently risen, we again started. The night was beautiful, and the rocks and mountains, towering up from the river's brink, looked grand, by the moonlight, as we passed along. The next day the heat of the sun was excessive, and we did not reach Trienna till one o'clock in the afternoon.

"Here we were all strangers. I had, however, a letter from Dr. Campbell to a young gentleman, which I delivered. He obtained a carriage, but Catharine was too weak to ride in it. How to procure people enough, in this land of strangers, to carry her in a litter to Dr. C.'s, a distance of five miles, I knew not. But our situation becoming known, men were soon at hand to carry her, free of all expense.

"And here I would observe, that every person, who saw her, was, so far as I could discover, much interested in her behalf.

"When we were ready to start, our young friend, to whom I brought the letter, placed the mother and sister of Catharine in the carriage, and went himself with them. Thus we were assisted on our way, the Lord putting it into the hearts of strangers to afford us every facility in their power, and we arrived at Dr. Campbell's, a little before dark, on the 27th."

Here, not less than at her father's house, she found friends, who were ready to make any sacrifice for her comfort, and with whom she could freely converse on the subject, which lay nearest her heart. Under the skilful care of Dr. Campbell, she soon began to amend, and hopes were entertained that she would even partially recover.

Early in June, her dear friend, Mrs. Potter, came from Creek-Path to see her.

This lady, in a letter to the Corresponding Secretary of the American Board, says: "She then seemed to think she might recover; but manifested no wish to live, unless it should be for the glory of God. She said, 'When I enjoy the presence of the Saviour, I long to be gone.'

"While at Dr. Campbell's, I wrote a letter to her brother David, informing him of her illness. When about to close the letter, I went to her bed-side and said, 'Catharine, what shall I say to your brother for you?'

"After a short pause, she replied, 'If you will write, I will dictate a short letter.'

"Then raising herself in the bed, and wiping away a tear, that was falling from her eye, she, with a sweet smile, began to relate what God had done for her soul while upon that sick bed.

"To my partial eye, she was, at that moment, an interesting spectacle, and I have often wished, that her portrait could then have been taken. Her countenance was softened with the affectionate remembrance of an endeared brother; her cheek was a little flushed with the exertion of speaking, her eye beamed with spiritual joy, and a heavenly smile animated the whole scene. I shall never forget it, nor the words she then whispered in my ear."

The reader will naturally desire to see the letter, which was dictated and penned under circumstances so interesting. It was written in exact accordance with her dictation, and was as follows.

Limestone, June 13, 1823.

My dear Brother,

Mrs. Potter has told you the particulars of my illness. I will only tell you what I have experienced on my sick-bed.

I have found, that it is good for me to be afflicted. The Saviour is very precious to me. I often enjoy his presence, and I long to be where I can enjoy it without sin. I have indeed been brought very low, and did not expect to live until this time. But I have had joy, such as I never experienced before. I longed to be gone; was ready to die at any moment.

I love you very much, and it would be a great happiness to me to see you again in this world. Yet I don't know that I shall. God only knows. We must submit to his will. We know, that if we never meet again in this world, the Lord has prepared a place in his heavenly kingdom, where I trust we shall meet, never to part. We ought to be thankful for what he has done for us. If he had not sent us the Gospel, we should have died without any knowledge of the Saviour.

You must not be grieved, when you hear of my illness. You must remember, that this world is not our home, that we must all die soon.

I am here under the care of Dr. Campbell, and his very kind family. My mother and sister Susan are with me. Since I came here, I have been a great deal better, and the doctor sometimes gives encouragement of my getting well. But we cannot tell. I am willing to submit myself to the will of God. I am willing to die, or live, as he sees best.

I know I am his. He has bought me with his blood, and I do not wish to have any will but his. He is good, and can do nothing wrong. I trust, if he spares my life, he will enable me to be faithful to his cause. I have no desire to live in this world, but to be engaged in his service.

It was my intention to instruct the people more than I had done, when I returned from Brainerd; but when I got home, I was not able to do it.

It was a great trial to me not to be able to visit our neighbours, and instruct them. But I feel that it is all right. It is my prayer that you may be useful, and I hope the Lord *will* make you useful to our poor people.

From your affectionate sister

CATHARINE.

How much soever her hopes, and those of her friends were raised at this period, with respect to her recovery, they were of brief duration. Though every attention, which an unwearied kindness could bestow, was given her, and prayer was offered continually on her behalf, her Lord and Master was pleased to hasten her departure. She had entered the last six weeks of her life, and thenceforward her descent towards the grave, was regular and unremitted.

Dr. Campbell now thought it his duty to inform her parents and herself, that his hopes, even of her partial recovery, were gone.

Upon communicating this intelligence to her father, who a little before had come to Limestone, the good old man, after a solemn silence of several minutes, observed, "The Lord has been good to give me such a child, and he has a right to take her when he thinks best. But though it is my duty to give her up, it is hard to part with her."

Catharine received the notice without manifesting the least alarm, only requesting the doctor to inform her, how long she might probably live.

On the morning of July 17th, she was supposed to have commenced her last agonies, and Dr. Campbell was immediately called to her bed-side.

"I found," says he, "some appearance of anxiety on her countenance, which was the result of new sensations of bodily distress, and not of any agitation of mind. As soon as she could speak, (for she was sometimes speechless,) extending her hand to me, she calmly observed, 'I am gone.'

"Some hours after this, when her distress returned, and her respiration became very difficult and painful, she said, in reference to her sufferings, 'What shall I do?' I inquired, if, in this trying hour, she could not confidently rely on her Saviour? She answered, 'Yes.'

"Through the day her mind was perfectly tranquil, and though several times, when her mother and friends were weeping about her, the tears would start into her eyes, she would quickly suppress them. She seemed to spend most of the time in prayer.

"The night was one of considerable distress, owing to her difficult of breathing. In the morning she looked toward the window, and asked me if it was not day. I replied, that it was. She then turned her eyes towards heaven, and an indescribable placidness spread over her countenance.

"Perhaps she thought, that the next morning she should behold, would be the morning of the resurrection.

"As death advanced, and the powers of nature gave way, she frequently offered her hand to the friends around her bed. Her mother and sister weeping over her, she looked steadily at the former, for a short time, filial love beaming from her eyes; and then,—she closed them in the sleep of death.

"She expired without a groan, or a struggle. Even those around the bed scarcely knew, that the last breath had left her, until I informed them she was gone.

"Thus fell asleep this lovely saint, in the arms of her Saviour, a little past 6 o'clock, on the morning of July 18th, 1823."

Her afflicted relatives conveyed her remains to Creek-Path, where they were, on the 20th, deposited near the residence of her parents, and by the side of her brother John, who had died about a year and a half before, in the triumphs of the same faith.

Her age was about twenty-three; and six years had elapsed from her first entering the school at Brainerd. She was then a heathen. But she became enlightened and sanctified, through the instrumentality of the Gospel of Jesus, preached to her by the missionaries of the cross; and her end was glorious.

A neat monument of wood, erected by her bereaved relatives, covers the grave where she was laid. And though, a few years hence, this monument may no longer exist to mark the spot where she slumbers, yet shall her dust be precious in the eyes of the Lord, and her virtues shall be told for a memorial of her.

CHAPTER VI.

HER CHARACTER.

Her mental characteristics.—Her attainments in intellectual and moral science.—Changes in her affections.—Her Christian conduct.—CONCLUSION.—The excellencies in her character a result of missionary labour.—How much can be made of the Indian character.—Grounds of encouragement.—Importance of present efforts.—Civilization never precedes Christianity.—The life of Catharine an appeal to the community.

A SUMMARY view will now be taken of the character of Catharine Brown, as it is exhibited in the documents, which have been the basis of the preceding memoir.

I. HER MENTAL CHARACTERISTICS.

The mind of Catharine was of a delicate texture, well proportioned, and happily balanced. Its perception was clear, its judgment correct, and it was well endued with that invaluable quality in the intellectual economy, good sense. In the acquisition of knowledge, it moved easily, and, considering her circumstances and health, wrought with success. In communicating to others what she knew, she had, owing to the clearness of her apprehensions, more than common felicity.

And who has not remarked her delicate sensibility, her exact views of dignity and propriety, her high principles of action, and her gentleness and sweetness of manner? With her advantages of person, and her excellencies of mind, she needed only greater opportunities, to have attained that high degree of refinement and grace, which is so much admired in the more elegant portion of civilized society.

But, until she came to the age, at which the females of our nation have nearly, or quite, completed their education, she derived no benefit whatever from the perusal of books, and enjoyed very little intercourse with civilized people. Her mind, like the wilderness in which she had her home, was uncultivated. But a small degree of intellectual, and scarcely any moral truth, had enlightened it. Bacon, and Newton, and Locke, and St. Paul, and a multitude of others possessing powerful intellects, who had brought the grandest truths in the natural and moral worlds within the comprehension of infantile genius, had, so far as she was concerned, lived in vain. In short, even at that late period, she had every thing to learn.

She lived but six years after her admission to the school at Brainerd. A desire for knowledge evidently brought her there; and that same desire, strengthened and sanctified by grace, attended her through life.

II. HER ATTAINMENTS.

1. Concerning those attainments, which are *not of a moral nature*, it will be needless to enter into a lengthened specification. It may, indeed, be impossible for us, into whose minds knowledge has been industriously poured from our earliest years, to form a just conception of her intellectual state, before she had access to the ordinary sources of information, or to ascertain, with precision, what revolutions occurred in her apprehensions of things. But there can be no doubt that most, even of the elements of learning, came before her in the garb of novelty, and that the field of her vision expanded, till she at length found herself introduced into quite a different sphere, from that, which had interested the curiosity of her opening youth.

It is affecting to think of the great mental changes, which were necessary, even to place her on a level with the ordinary intelligence of civilized life. But it is delightful to contemplate these changes as more than accomplished. To a few of the more important of them the attention of the reader is, for a moment, invited.

Her acquaintance with the *geographical features of the earth*, must have been exceedingly vague and limited, hardly extending beyond the wilderness, that embosomed her father's house. After her introduction to the missionaries, that acquaintance was extended to the great natural divisions of the world, its physical aspect, and its civil departments.

Her *astronomical* views, untutored as she was, may easily be conjectured. But she was instructed to contemplate worlds and suns and systems, in uncounted numbers, wheeling, at the command of their Creator, through immensity.

Her apprehensions respecting the *human race* were so imperfect, that she supposed her own people a distinct order of beings. But soon she learns, that God "hath made of one blood all nations of men."

How exceedingly confined, also, how next to nothing, must have been her knowledge of *history*. Ages that were past, must have been to her almost as much a blank, as ages that were to come. But soon the Bible, the wisest, most sure, most comprehensive history of man, is placed in her hands; and she has besides, access to a variety of the most useful human compends. Being thus favoured, it may well be presumed, that the more interesting events of antiquity rose, in rapid succession, above her mental horizon.

Such changes as these elevate the mind immeasurably above the standard of the mere child of nature, and, when beheld in any human soul, must be, to a philanthropist, a subject of grateful contemplation.

2. The greatest and infinitely the most important acquisitions of Catharine, however, had respect to *moral* subjects,—to God, and a future state, to the character, duty and highest interest of

man, and the provisions made for his salvation. On all subjects of this class, her ideas, when she came to Brainerd, were very confused and imperfect; and in regard to some of the most momentous of them, she was in total ignorance. She went there an untutored pagan. Scarcely a ray of moral light had gleamed upon her soul. The visible creation was indeed open and bright before her. But how little of the divine perfections does fallen man discern there, until they are pointed out by the finger of revelation!

Of the *moral perfections of God,* such as his holiness, justice, and goodness, she had no conceptions at all, when she entered the mission school. Her knowledge of God, like that of most of her countrymen, was confined almost to the narrowest possible limits. *Galunlahtiahi*, or *the Great Being above*, was thought to possess a material form, and his most prominent attribute to be physical strength. The Indian languages are said to have no word that signifies *spirit*, nor the pagan Indians any idea of a spiritual substance. The spirituality of Jehovah, his holy character, his love of holiness, his hatred of sin, the strictness of his law, his righteous government over the world, and his illimitable benevolence, were things of which Catharine knew little, or nothing.

But soon we find her mind richly furnished with all these views of God. His moral perfections arrest her attention, and she sees, in all their exhibitions, a lovely and attractive glory. What new views of the Eternal must they have been, which drew forth such language as this:—"O, he is good, kind, merciful." "I feel it is good to be afflicted, knowing that the Lord is good, and will always do what is right." "I thank God, I am entirely in his hands." "The Lord's will be done, and not mine." "O happy day, when God himself shall be my joy!" No heathen ever used such language as this. It springs only from the illuminations of Christianity.

Of the *Lord Jesus Christ* she had no knowledge, when introduced to the missionaries; and when told of him, for the first time, she supposed, that what he had done for sinners had no reference to her, or her people.

But the united testimony of all is, that, after her conversion, the SAVIOR was her favourite theme of contemplation and discourse. He was her ALPHA and OMEGA, her ALL IN ALL. His person, character, and work, appeared to her amazingly interesting. How often does she express a desire to know him better, to love him more, to be more grateful for what he has done, to do more in return, to be with him, to see him, and to sing his praises. "O," she exclaims, "how delightful is the view of my Saviour." "He is precious to me. I often enjoy his presence. I long to be where I can enjoy him without sin." "He has bought me with his blood, and I wish not to have any will of my own. He is good, and can do nothing wrong."

And what new views did she acquire, with regard to the *people* of God. At first, she thought them unhappy, and was fearful they would render her unhappy. But soon she thinks them the happiest people in the world, and longs for their society more than for that of any others. With them she wishes to live, with them to die, with them to be forever. What amount of earthly good would have induced her to forego their company, for a single year, and cast her lot among the giddy sons and daughters of fashionable pleasure?

"i cannot," she remarks, "express how much I love the missionaries with whom I live. I feel not my privileges, until I am away from them, and mingle with worldly people. Then I long to get back, and be with Christians." "I often think of the glorious day, when I shall meet all good missionaries in the kingdom of our Saviour. I shall then be always with those dear friends, who have told me so much about heaven, and taught me to love and serve Christ." "O, happy day, when I shall see all the Christians, who have ever lived."

We also perceive a great alteration in her views of *herself*. She has declared, that when she came to Brainerd, she did not know she was a sinner; and we are informed, that she was vain of her person, vain of her decorations, and satisfied with herself.

Yet what self-abasing views had she, ever after her conversion. "I see nothing," she observes, "to trouble me, but my wicked heart. It appears to me, that the more I wish to serve God, the more I sin. I seem never to have done any thing good in the sight of God."

"Humility," says Mrs. Potter, "was the most conspicuous trait in her character. I never could discover, that her vanity was excited by the numerous attentions, which she received from different parts of our country. She received them as paid her for Christ's sake. When presents came, her language was, 'These do not belong to me. I do not deserve them. Many Christians have heard, that I love the Saviour, and send me presents on this account. But oh, I feel ashamed that I live so far from him.'

"She received many letters, some of which were highly complimentary, but so far from fostering pride, they always seemed to increase her humility. Once, having received a letter full of expressions of the strongest admiration of her character, she was gently cautioned against being lifted up with vanity. The tears started into her eyes, and she replied, 'I do not wish to be proud;' and added, 'that she believed people had formed too high an opinion of her, and that is they knew her personally, their esteem would be diminished.'

"She was much distressed, that so many of her letters had been published, and, for a season, it was with difficulty, that we could persuade her to write to her correspondents. 'I suppose,' she said, 'the object at *first* was, to show that an Indian could improve. But two or three letters would have answered this purpose, as well as all I have ever written.' "[11]

Mr. Leech says, "I have often seen her in company at Huntsville, and although she was very much caressed, and her society sought, by the most respectable people, yet she always

---

[11] Her letters were published, by different friends to whom they were addressed, to gratify the laudible curiosity of the community. It is proper to remark, however, that not more than two or three were ever inserted in the publications of the American Board.

appeared humble. There was nothing about her, that was vain, or assuming. This was not the effect of insensibility to those acts of kindness. She would sometimes say to her particular friends. 'I wish I was more worthy of such friendly attentions.' "

Observe, too, what a revolution was effected in her views of *this world*. An Indian's heaven, even when most distinctly apprehended, has fewer points of attraction, than the earth. Catharine, on coming to Brainerd, evidently regarded it, when she thought of it at all, as a remote, obscure, undefined something, more to be dreaded, than desired. Hence her imagination had contemplated whatever is lovely and attractive, as shining forth only in this world. If she made any comparisons, they only deepened the conviction, that earthly objects were most desirable.

But after her conversion, what a change! Her contemplations are elevated to a superior world of realities. She learns of a higher state of existence, designed for the good of the human race; where the inhabitants are all holy, their employments holy, their joys holy; where the disorders and miseries of earth are not known; where "there shall be no more death, neither sorrow, nor crying, neither shall there be any more pain;" and where there is "no need of the sun, neither of the moon, to shine in it, for the glory of God doth lighten it, and the Lamb is the light thereof." Now, her views of the world are changed. The contrast of earthly with heavenly things, and of the creature with God, hath spoiled the glories of the world.

"How vain," she says, "does this world appear in my eyes. It is nothing but vanity and sin." "Sweet and reviving is the thought, that I am not to continue long in this world, but hope soon to rest in the city of my God." "When I enjoy the presence of my Saviour, I long to be gone." "How happy shall I feel, when I land on the shores of eternal felicity."

To proceed farther in this analysis, is unnecessary. Enough has been said to illustrate the changes, which occurred in her apprehensions on moral subjects. She seems to have possessed much of that kind of understanding, which is denominated, in the word of God, a "spiritual understanding." She appears to have received a spiritual discernment, which enabled her, by the simple reading of the Scriptures, meditation and prayer, to acquire a knowledge of the hidden glories of spiritual things. Hence, the spiritual world, which had been concealed before her conversion, was to her, ever after, a world of beauties, upon which she loved to dwell.

III. CHANGES IN HER AFFECTIONS.

The objects of all human affections may be divided into two grand classes, which are designated, in the divine word, as *things earthly*, and *things heavenly*. The earthly things, are the riches, honours, and pleasures of the world. The heavenly things, are whatever bear the marks of a heavenly origin, or of a heavenly destination; such as God, and holy beings, and sacred truth.

When Catharine first became acquainted with the missionaries, her affections were resting wholly on the former class of objects. But how much evidence is there, that, before her decease, there was almost an entire transfer of her affections; that they rested almost wholly on heavenly things.

With respect to the general character of her religious affections, it may be remarked, that they were uniformly tender, often lively, but never enthusiastic. Dr. Campbell observes, "that she never appeared to receive the Christian system of faith otherwise than on the force of evidence, and that evidence drawn from the Bible. The extravagance of feeling, which is the effect chiefly of animal excitement, she could not comprehend, but felt satisfied with possessing that holiness of heart, which lends to supreme love to God."—"She was never enthusiastic," says Mrs. Potter, "yet had seasons of exalted joy, when, to use her own language, 'she felt as though she was in heaven, and was disappointed, when her thoughts returned to earth, and she found herself here!' She had, also, seasons of deep sorrow of heart, when she mourned the hidings of her Saviour's countenance, and groaned under the pressure of indwelling sin."

Catharine possessed nothing of that stoical insensibility to pleasure, or pain, for which the Indian character has been considered remarkable. There was never any thing in her deportment like unfeeling hardihood. The very reverse of this was true. She had a heart for friendship, for sympathy, for tender emotion. This is apparent in all her writings, and in her whole history; and is amply confirmed by her intimate friend and companion, Mrs. Potter. She remarks, "Catharine possessed a heart, that could feel for another's wo, and rejoice in another's prosperity."

To the *Saviour* her love was uncommonly strong, and continued so, in every variety of circumstance. Who has not been impressed with this, while reading her journal, her letters, and her recorded sayings, and while contemplating the events of her life? Love to the Saviour, was her ruling principle. She knew his voice. She delighted to sit as his feet. She was overwhelmed with wonder at his condescending goodness. She was enraptured at the thought of beholding his face. Hear her own words. "I will go wherever the Saviour calls me." "How good it is to lie at the feet of Jesus." "O how good is he in permitting me to partake of his grace." "Sweet is the thought of soon beholding the face of the Redeemer."

Here again Dr. Campbell will be quoted. "The Saviour seemed to be continually the anchor of her hope, the source of her constant and greatest happiness, and the object of her most ardent love. With her friends, she was at all times communicative and interesting; but when He became the theme of conversation, the faculties of her soul appeared to receive new vigour, and she became doubly interesting. Every expression shewed, that she was charmed with the goodness of God, in making such provision for fallen, lost man. Although on other subjects she was not generally very animated, her whole soul seemed to feel the importance of this, which produced an earnestness of expression and manner, that constrained those around her to feel its importance too."

Hence she felt, and uniformly manifested, a deep interest in the *cause of Christ*. Especially did she long to have her own people savingly acquainted with the Lord Jesus. For this object chiefly she wished to live. This made her almost unwilling to die. "My heart bleeds for my poor people," was her language; "I am determined to pray for them, while God lends me breath."

Her biographer might enlarge, upon her dependence on God, which led her beautifully to say, "I am a child, I can do nothing; but in God will I trust, for I know there is no one else, to whom can I look for help." He might speak of her tender affection for her friends; of her gratitude for favours shewn her; and of her compassion for the world at large. But enough has been said to shew, that she possessed much, very much of the meek and glowing benevolence of the Gospel.

> "Fair spirit, nurs'd in forest wild,
> Where caught thy breast those sacred flames?"

IV. HER CHRISTIAN CONDUCT.

There is no reason to believe, that any thing in the conduct of Catharine ever approached to what is denominated immoral. And this is very remarkable, considering her early circumstances. Yet, until she came to Brainerd, she was not religious. She did not lead a life of piety. Till then, the only tendency of her mind and heart and conduct, was towards the world. As she neither knew, nor loved "those things which are above," so neither did she seek them.

But a change occurred in her objects of pursuit; a revolution took place in the general course and tenor of her life. We find new aims, new plans, new habits of action. "Old things are passed away."

CATHARINE BROWN

Her *habits of devotion* might well render her an example to others. Not only did she delight to be present in the public assembly, not only did she love to gather little circles of her Cherokee friends for social prayer, but she was constant and earnest in her more private approaches to her God and Saviour.

Mrs. Potter observes; "The Bible, was her constant companion. The law of God was her delight and meditation all the day. And I think I may safely say, that no morning, or evening passed, during her residence with us, (which was considerably more than a year,) when she did not retire to hold communion with her God. At these seasons of devotion, I was not unfrequently permitted to be by her side, and listen to the fervent breathings of her soul. In strains of the deepest humility, she confessed her sins, acknowledged her obligations to her heavenly Father, and with great fervency prayed for complete conformity to the divine will. Her dear people were never forgotten, and her petitions were extended from them to all mankind."

Her *zeal* was not an irregular, evanescent flame. It was permanent, and always active. How faithful, laborious, and successful she was, with respect to her own family, has been noticed in the preceding memoir. A more kind, attentive, and obliging daughter and sister, than was Catharine Brown, or one more faithfully solicitous for the spiritual good of her relatives, is scarcely to be found, it is believed, in any civilized land.

Nor was she ever unmindful of the duties she owed her people, and she seems to have closely watched for opportunities to do them good. Indeed, their conversion to God was her favourite object, to which she clung, with unyielding tenacity, through ever vicissitude of health and circumstance, down to the hour of her dissolution.

"Patient she strives,
By prayer, and by instruction, to arouse
Reflection in the hearts of those she styles
Her wretched people. Modest, tender, kind
Her words and actions; every vain desire
Is laid obedient at the feet of Christ.

> And now no more the gaiety she seeks
> Of proud apparel; ornaments of gold
> She gladly barters for the plain attire
> Of meek and lowly spirits."[12]

It cannot be forgotten by the reader, how diligently she pursued her studies, both at Brainerd and at Creek-Path, in order that she might be more eminently fitted for usefulness; nor how meekly she bore those acquisitions, which elevated her above every other female of her tribe.

That there were defects in her Christian character, must be presumed, in the absence of positive proof, from analogy. The best Christians have failings. But what were hers? The materials for this memoir were furnished by a considerable number of persons, who knew her well; and, without seeming to have been conscious of the omission, not one of them has specified a single fault in her character, as a Christian. Mrs. P. has simply said, that she was not entirely free from the inadvertences of youth. It would seem, therefore, and there is reason to believe it was the fact, that her failings, whatever they might be, were not such as are apt to make a strong impression on the mind.

"Through faith in the Lord Jesus," says the first spiritual guide she ever had, the Rev. Mr. Kingsbury, "she was enabled to bring forth the fruits of righteousness, has left a bright example of the power of divine grace over one who was born in the darkness of heathenism, and is now rejoicing with her Saviour."

CONCLUSION.

SUCH was Catharine Brown, the converted Cherokee. Such, too, were the changes wrought in her, through the blessing of Almighty God on the labours of Missionaries. They, and only they, as the instruments of divine grace, had the formation of her

---

[12] Traits of the Aborigines of America, pp. 161, 162.

CATHARINE BROWN

Christian character; and that character, excellent and lovely as it was, resulted from the nature of their instructions. Her expansion of mind her enlargement of views, her elevated affections, her untiring benevolence, are all to be traced, under God, to her intercourse with them. The glory belongs to God; but the instrumental agency, the effective labour, the subordinate success, were theirs.

In her history, we see how much can be made of the Indian character. Catharine was an Indian. She might have said, as her brother did to thousands, while passing through these States, "Aboriginal blood flows through my veins." True, it was not unmixed; but the same may be affirmed of many others of her people. Her parentage, her early circumstances and education, with a few unimportant exceptions, were like those of the Cherokees generally. She dwelt in the same wilderness, was conversant with the same society, was actuated by the same fears, and hopes, and expectations, and naturally possessed the same traits of character. Yet what did she become! How agreeable as an associate, how affectionate as a friend, how exemplary as a member of the domestic and social circle and of the Christian church, how blameless and lovely in all the walks of life! Her Christian character was esteemed by all who knew her, while she lived, and will bear the strictest scrutiny, now she is dead. To such an excellence may the Indian character attain; for, to such an excellence did it actually attain in her.

And why may it not arrive at the same excellence, in other Indians? Are there no other minds among them as susceptible of discipline and culture? no other spirits, that, in the plastic hands of the Divine Agent, can receive as beautiful a conformation? Are there not dispositions as gentle, hearts as full of feeling, minds as lively and strong? And cannot such minds be so fashioned and adorned, that heavenly grace shall beam as charmingly from them, as it did from hers?

The supposition, that she possessed mental and moral capabilities, which are rare among her people, while it adds nothing to our respect for her, does injustice to her nation. In personal attraction, and in universal propriety of manner, she was, undoubtedly, much distinguished. But, in amiableness of disposition, in quickness of apprehension, in intellectual vigour, it is believed there are hundreds of Cherokee youth, who are scarcely less favoured.

In confirmation of this, will be given the description of a school, composed entirely of young Cherokees, from the pen of a clergyman, whose accuracy of judgment, and faithfulness of description, have never been questioned.

"It has never been according to our views of propriety and expediency to be lavish in commendations of our schools; lest we should seem to colour high and exaggerate, or to indulge in pride and vain glory. We think, however. (and we would ever think soberly,) that much might be said in favour of the schools at Dwight, without in any measure departing from "words of truth and soberness." I would not draw invidious comparisons, between the schools here and those of other similar institutions. But I would say, that I never saw, at any place, in any country, more interesting groups of children, than those at present under our care: interesting, in almost every point of view, whether we consider them in their relations, their appearance, their behavior, their progress, or their prospects.

"Those, who, when revolving in their thoughts the idea of Indians and savages, vainly imagine that nothing can belong to the aborigines of our country, except what is frightful in appearance, and deeply imbued with cruelty and barbarism, would scarcely believe themselves to be in an Indian school, when surrounded by the children, which fill our little sylvan seminary. Were they here, they would see nothing of that coarseness of feature, nor ferocity of look, nothing like that dirty dress, ugly visage, and repelling countenance, and nothing of that hard, unkind, and cruel disposition, which they have been wont to associate with the Indian character. But they would see a lovely group of children, who, by the regularity of their features, their neat and cleanly drew, their fair complexions, (fair indeed for a sultry clime,) their orderly and becoming behavior, their intelligence and sprightliness, their mildness of disposition, tempered with a manly spirit, and their progress in knowledge, would not suffer by a comparison with most schools in a civilized land, nor disgrace respectable parents, by passing as their sons and daughters.

"Such, dear Sir, are our schools at Dwight, our precious children, not long since brought from the shades of the forest. We love them, and we can but love them, for they are lovely. They are docile in their dispositions, generally quick in their apprehensions, prompt in their obedience, active and sprightly in their sports, and diligent and ambitious in their studies. Of the whole number of sixty, who compose the school in two departments, there are not more than six who cannot read with ease in the New Testament, and spell almost any words put to them. A considerable number can read with propriety and apparent understanding any book, and write a fair and legible hand. Near one fourth of both departments of the school are pursuing the study of geography. Some of the boys have made some progress in grammar and arithmetic, and in some other branches. It may be said with truth, that most, if not all, are as forward as the children of most district schools in the most favoured part of New England. But what is more interesting to the Christian is their intelligent reading of the Scriptures, singing with delightful voices the praises of God, and making progress in a knowledge of the Gospel."[13]

The uniform testimony respecting all the other schools, which have been established by the American Board, is in accordance with the above.

Catharine was not the only convert from her people. There have been others, both among the old and the young, in whom similar transformations have been wrought. Her brother John was an instance. Her aged and venerable parents, who are much and justly respected by all who know them, are instances. Others still might be named, were it not probable that these pages will fall under their notice. More than fifty Cherokees were added to the church, the first year after the decease of Catharine, the great proportion of whom adorn their profession in a manner resembling what we admire in her.

It is hardly possible, indeed, that any of these converts should become so well known to our community, as she was. Circumstances have changed. The novelty of Indian missions is gone. The multiplication of converts diminishes our curiosity respecting individuals. But excellence and worth of character, are none the less real for being unnoticed and unknown.

Here, then, we find encouragement. The success of past efforts has been rich in its nature, and animating in its amount; and the same kind of instruments, increased in number, are still employed, and employed, too, upon similar materials. The course of divine grace, moreover, is, in some sense, uniform, like the course of nature; so that what Almighty God has done, in past time, is an earnest and a pledge (circumstances being the same,) of what he will do, in time to come. Upon these accounts, among others, we may cherish raised expectations. Should the enterprise, which has been commenced so auspiciously, be prosecuted with prudence, zeal, and in the fear

---

[13] Missionary Herald, vol. xx, pp. 345, 346.

of God, we shall not be extravagant if we look for the general prevalence of pure religion among a people, in the midst of whom, at the breaking up of their long night of paganism, this interesting female shone as a morning star.

The present is emphatically the time for vigorous Christian effort. Probably it is the only time when great success is possible. Various unpropitious causes press heavily upon the poor Indians; and it is believed, that nothing will save them from extinction, as a people, but the general prevalence of true religion. All things else will be vain without this.

The position, that civilization must precede Christianity, is so unsupported by facts, is so opposed to all experience, that one would think it could hardly be advanced by enlightened philosophers, or be received by rational Christians. What is civilization? In Pagan and Mohammedan countries, it is, it ever has been, a state of society, where moral excellence is little known, and domestic and social happiness little enjoyed; where man is a lordly tyrant, and woman is a slave. True civilization is found only in Christian countries; and no where, but as the *result* of Christianity; of Christianity, too, planted, in the first instance, by missionary enterprise.

Bring this religion to act strongly upon the Indians. Give them the full enjoyment of Christian ordinances. Then their 'winter will be past, the rain will be over and gone.' Agriculture, art, science, legislation, and literature, the germs of which already appear, will grow in rich luxuriance, and the Indian character will be respected by the nations of the earth.

Let the life of Catharine Brown operate as an appeal to the benevolence of the Christian community. Though dead, she speaks: and oh, let her voice fall with persuasive and irresistible eloquence upon every ear.

Shall her people, of whom, by the purifying and ennobling influences of the Gospel, so much can be made, be abandoned to ignorance and wo? Shall beings, who are capable of knowing God, of understanding the grand economy of his grace, of enjoying the imperishable blessings of his salvation, be shut out eternally for such wisdom, and debarred forever from such enjoyment?

Are they not susceptible of whatever is useful, and beautiful, and even sublime, in character? Can they not appreciate, and will they not use, the means of Christian civilization, if placed within their reach?

And may we not expect an abundant reward? Nay, have we not already been amply rewarded? To say nothing of the impulse given to the intellect, the industry, and the enterprise, of the nation, to which the subject of this memoir belonged; or of their accelerated progress in legislation and government; or of the amelioration in the habits and manners of their domestic and social life; or of the rudiments of learning imparted to a multitude of children and youth; or of the amount of sacred truth, the only means of conversion and sanctification, instilled into their minds; or of an inheritance in the heavens secured to many souls:—to say nothing of all this, Were not the holy life and triumphant death of Catharine Brown, an ample remuneration for all the labours and expenditures of the mission to her tribe?

Say, ye missionaries of the cross, should ye repent of your self-denying toils, if this had proved your only reward? Say, ye churches of the Redeemer, would ye recal her sainted spirit from the skies, if what ye have expended for her nation could be refunded? A thousand worlds would not be worth what you have, through the grace of God, secured to her, as is humbly believed, in the regions of the blessed. And when ye, also, stand on the heights of the Zion above, and behold her ransomed spirit "filled with all the fulness of God," and exulting amid the hosts of heaven, well ye have any regrets for the sacrifices it cost you to send the Gospel to her people?

O let sloth be driven away; let the grasp of avarice be loosened; let benevolence assume the dominion; let a spirit of enterprise be kindled; let the messengers of salvation be quickly sent to every tribe that roams the western wilds.

MEMOIR OF

Then "the wilderness and the solitary place shall be glad for them, and the desert shall rejoice and blossom as the rose."

FINIS.

Book II

THE

LITTLE

OSAGE CAPTIVE,

An Authentic Narrative

BY ELIAS CORNELIUS.

I asked, what had become of her parents? When one of them went to his sack and took from it TWO SCALPS! "Here" said he,"they are"; holding them up in his hand before me.

THE LITTLE OSAGE CAPTIVE,

AN

Authentic Narrative.

BY ELIAS CORNELIUS.

BOSTON:
SAMUEL T. ARMSTRONG AND CROCKER & BREWSTER.
NEW YORK: JOHN P. HAVEN.
1822.

DISTRICT OF MASSACHUSETTS, *to wit:*
District Clerk's Office.

BE IT REMEMBERED, that on the first day of March, A. D. 1822, and in the forty-sixth year of the Independence of the United States of America, Samuel T. Armstrong, of the said district, has deposited in this office, the title of a book, the right whereof he claims as proprietor, in the words following, to wit:

"The Little Osage Captive, an authentic narrative; by Elias Cornelius."

In conformity to the act of the Congress of the United States, intitled, "An act for the encouragement of learning, by securing the copies of maps, charts and books, to the authors and proprietors of such copies, during the times therein mentioned;" and also to an act intitled, "An act supplementary to an act, intitled an act for the encouragement of learning, by securing the copies of maps, charts and books, to the authors and proprietors of such copies during the times therein mentioned; and extending the benefits thereof to the arts of designing, engraving and etching historical and other prints."

JNO. W. DAVIS,
Clerk of the District of Massachusetts.

ADVERTISEMENT.

It having been stated, in the notice for publishing the Little Osage Captive, that the work would be accompanied with "several cuts;" it may appear strange that it should have been issued with but *two* engravings. The reason is, that when that notice was given, it was expected the engravings would be prepared on *wood*, instead of *copper*, as has been the fact. The latter, it is well known, are more expensive than the former, and being capable of a much finer execution—are esteemed more valuable. It was thought that a smaller number prepared in this way would be more acceptable than a larger number prepared in the other.

PREFACE.

IN the year 1817 the writer of the following narrative, was employed by the American Board of Commissioners for Foreign Missions, to visit several tribes of Indians, residing in the south western parts of the United States. The object of the mission, was to converse with the natives and obtain their consent to have schools, and other institutions, established among them, for the purpose of instructing them in Christianity, and the most useful arts of civilized life.

While performing the duties of this appointment, the principal incidents occurred, which are related in this little history. The facts which it contains, are derived from the author's own knowledge; or from the testimony of persons of undoubted veracity. Some of them have been published already, and have awakened a lively interest in the religious community. But, as they were imperfectly known, and lay scattered through several volumes of missionary intelligence, it was conceived that they might be put into the form of a continued narrative, and be so combined with other facts not hitherto published, as to make a useful and entertaining memoir.

Such a memoir, it was thought, would be especially interesting to children and youth; and would serve to direct their attention to those efforts which are made to enlighten and convert the heathen. By the aid of parents and instructers, it might perhaps, help to enkindle their seal in the missionary

PREFACE.

cause; and prompt them to those *early habits* of exertion, in supporting it, which are the sure means of its future prosperity.

It was the hope of interesting this class of persons, chiefly, which led the writer to the present undertaking. He believes that the time has come, when new, and unparalleled exertions, must be made to propagate the Gospel. The present generation will do little more than begin the work. To the rising generation, and the generations to come, it must be left to carry on and complete it.

It is impossible, therefore, to say, how much is depending upon the direction which is now given, on this subject, to the minds of children and youth. The views and prepossessions of early life, are not easily lost. Should these, for time to come, be in favor of missionary exertions, the result would be auspicious, beyond the power of present calculation. Let it every where be deeply impressed upon the minds of children and youth, that the wants of the heathen are pressing and great; and that it is the duty of all, who have the means, to send them the Gospel: let them, from the commencement of their rational existence, be taught to think much of the condition of the heathen, to commiserate their wretchedness, and to make frequent sacrifices for their benefit; and who can tell, what revolutions may be effected, in the moral state of mankind, within the course of another generation?

It becomes parents and teachers, and all, who have the management of youth, to ponder deeply the responsibility of their station, as it respects the interests of this great cause. It becomes every *mother* to consider it: and as she moulds the pliant mind of her infant child, to be careful to impress it, with a conviction of its superior excellence, and the strength of its claims to the support of every humane and benevolent person. Who knows, but upon her fidelity, may be pending the character and state of future millions, both for this world, and the next? Could the mother of the illustrious Washington have known, that the future instrument of her country's independence, was entrusted to her care; how would she have felt the motives to

PREFACE.

faithfulness increased? And shall not every pious mother now, be stimulated to unwearied diligence by the reflection, that the infant son whom she holds in her arms, may yet be enrolled with a Brainerd, or a Swartz; a Buchanan, or a Martyn?

Should this little book afford any aid, to those who are endeavoring to make an impression upon the rising generation, in favor of the missionary cause, the writer will not have labored in vain; and that this may be the effect of it, he would fervently commend it to the favor and blessing of God.

Salem, Massachusetts,
Feb. 1822.

THE

LITTLE OSAGE CAPTIVE

CHAPTER I.

The author is travelling in the wilderness. Meets a party of Indian warriors. Observes among them a little Indian girl. Is told that she is a captive, who has been taken in a war with another tribe. Her Indian owner shows him the scalps of her father and mother. The author entreats him to place her in the missionary school at Brainerd. He consents; and the author addresses a letter by him to Mr. Kingsbury.

THE little Indian girl, who is the subject of this narrative, was brought to notice by a remarkable interposition of Providence. In the autumn of 1817, I was travelling from Brainerd, a missionary station among the Cherokee Indians, to New Orleans. Early on the morning of Saturday, November 15th, as I was journeying on horseback, in company with three or four other persons, we came to a small stream which forms the eastern boundary of the Chickasaw tribe of Indians, and which the white people call, Caney-creek. It was in the wilderness, a few miles south of the Tennessee river, and about two hundred miles west from Brainerd.

As there are but few bridges in the country, travellers are, commonly, obliged to ford the streams;—or where the water is too deep to admit of this, they drive their horses into them and make them swim across; while they contrive to get over, upon logs, or in some other way.

When we arrived at Caney-creek, we found that we should be unable to cross, without much difficulty, as well as danger. A heavy rain had fallen, the day and night before, and had raised it to such a height, that its banks were overflown in many places; and every pit in the low grounds through which it runs, was filled with water. It was necessary, however, that we should proceed on our journey as rapidly as possible. The Sabbath was approaching; and we wished to observe it as a day of rest. There were no suitable accommodations for ourselves or our horses, where we were; and good accommodations, a few miles beyond. We spared no pains, therefore, to overcome the difficulties of our situation. But all was in vain. After toiling several hours, we were compelled to desist, and stay where we were, until the waters should subside.

Our disappointment was great: but Providence had wise and good ends to accomplish by our delay. Towards evening, a company of Indians arrived from the westward; and, being much more expert in the use of their horses than we were, succeeded in crossing the creek. They proved to be a party of Cherokees, returning from the country which had recently been ceded to them, by the Government of the United States, on the west side of the Mississippi river.

The country, which had thus been ceded, lies upon the North side of the Arkansaw river, about four hundred miles above its junction with the Mississippi. It had been given them, in exchange for other lands, belonging to their tribe, on the east side of that river. The Cherokees who emigrate there, are called Arkansaw Cherokees, to distinguish them from those who remain in their native country.

The party who have been mentioned, had been visiting their newly acquired territory; and were returning with the view of

OSAGE CAPTIVE.

taking their families thither, in the spring. As the object of my mission was to confer with the Indians, respecting the institution of schools, and other means of instruction, among them, I thought this a good opportunity to ascertain the feelings of the Arkansaw Cherokees on the subject; and accordingly walked to the place where the party had encamped for the night.

There were a dozen or more of them; and among them, one who could talk a little English. They had built a fire under a tall tree, which stood upon a gentle rise of ground, about half a mile from the creek. Some of them, were sitting upon the ground, and the rest were standing. Their baggage consisted of various articles of traveling furniture; some sacks of corn and other provisions; the skins of wild beasts with which they made their beds at night; several bunches of bows and arrows—which, together with their guns and tomahawks, were lying about promiscuously upon the ground, and presented a truly savage appearance.

The bows and arrows, with some other things, I learned had been taken from the Osage Indians, with whom they had been at war. Some of them were stained with blood, having been taken from the bodies of the killed or wounded.

These Osages are a large and powerful tribe, whose country extends from the waters of the Arkansaw, to those of the Missouri. They are divided into two nations; and are called the Osages of the Missouri, or the Osages of the Arkansaw, according as the country they inhabit, is in the neighborhood of one or the other of these rivers. It was with the *latter*, that the Cherokees had been to war; the country they occupy, lying contiguous to that which is claimed by the Osages of the Arkansaw.[1]

But, that which most of all attracted my attention, in the Indian group, I have described, was a little girl, apparently not more than five years old, who seemed to be travelling with them. She was the only female, and the only child, in the company.

---

[1] For an account of the origin of the war, See Appendix.

Thinking it strange that so young a person, should be travelling with a party of Indian warriors, I inquired whose child she was? They replied,—she was a captive, whom they had taken from the Osages in one of their late engagements. I asked, what had become of her parents? When one of them went to his sack, and took from it TWO SCALPS! "Here," said he, "they are;" holding them up in his hand before me. The poor child gazed at them with astonishment, as though she knew not what to make of it.

If ever I felt the deepest pity, it was when I beheld this unoffending prisoner. To the persons and language of those about her, she was an utter stranger. Her parents were dead; and such were the horrid memorials, by which the thought was to be kept alive in her memory. She had travelled with her new owners, more than five hundred miles through a dreary wilderness;—and knew not how much further she might have to go. The season was cold and rainy; and she had been exposed to all its inclemencies, without a shelter for nearly a month.

I went up to her, and attempted to take her into my arms; but immediately she began to cry. The Indians smiled, and said, she was afraid of me, because I was a *white man*. She had probably heard much of the cruelty and injustice of the white people, and had formed an idea that they were even worse than the Indians.

How much I wished she could know the feelings of my heart towards her. But she understood not my language, and there was no one present, who could converse with her, in her own. I endeavored, however, by treating her kindly, and using the tenderest, and most affectionate tones, when I spoke to her, to gain her confidence; and make her feel that I was her friend. I gave her some cake, and a bright little cup which I happened to have with me, and she took them with cheerfulness. The latter pleased her greatly; but with the former, she seemed not to know what to do. It was probably the first time, she has ever seen any food of this kind.

In her appearance, the little Osage captive was prettier than most children. She had, it is true, the copper-color which belongs to all the Indians of America; but her features were so regular; she had so much mildness and simplicity in her eye; and her strait, black hair, hung down so loosely about her neck, that one could not help calling her a handsome child. Her dress was poor, but better than Indian children of her age, are accustomed to wear. She had something like a bonnet, upon her head; and a loose woollen blanket, was wrapped around her, to shield her from the weather.

I now thought of nothing so much, as how I might obtain her deliverance from captivity. Understanding that an Indian in the company, had bought her of the original captor, by giving a horse for her, I addressed myself to him; and tried to get his consent to have her sent to Brainerd,—at this time called Chick-a-mau-gáh; where a missionary establishment had been made, and a school opened, for the education of Indian children. I assured him that she should be fed, and clothed, and instructed, free of expense to him; and intimated, that if he preferred it, the missionaries would bring her up as their own child, and pay him a reasonable price for her redemption.

Observing that he had an affection for the child, I appealed to his feelings: and represented to him on the one hand, the greatness of the calamity which she had met with; and on the other, how well it would be made up, by allowing her to live with the missionaries, who would be the kindest of fathers and mothers to her, and give her an education which might make her happy in this world, and in the world to come.

To my great satisfaction, he appeared to feel what I said; and consented, without much hesitation, to send her to the school soon after his return home. I then sat down, and wrote by him to the Rev. Cyrus Kingsbury, the superintendant of the establishment, desiring him to receive the orphan, and if possible, to redeem her. The price which her owner demanded, as nearly as I can recollect, was one hundred dollars. I knew, that it would be difficult for Mr. Kingsbury to advance so large a sum, consistently with other claims upon the Institution; but I had no doubt, the money would be refunded to him, the moment an appeal should be made to the public.

These arrangements being made, I took my leave of the Indians, and of the little Osage; and returned to the place where I had stopped for the night, with emotions which it would be difficult to describe. I could not help admiring the wisdom, and goodness of Providence, which seemed to have detained me here, on purpose that I might meet this company of Indians, and rescue, as I hoped, an unfortunate heathen child from captivity. The delay was contrary to my own intentions; and for a time, was a severe trial. But I now saw that it had been ordered in kindness, and felt sincerely thankful for it.

On the morrow, the waters of the creek had fallen, and I proceeded on my journey, with my companions, at an early hour. We had not advanced far before we met several other parties of Cherokees, more numerous than the first, returning from the Arkansaw country; among whom, we afterwards learned, were other captives. But we passed them without stopping, and had no opportunity to ascertain the fact. In a little time, we were at the place which we had labored so industriously to reach the day before; and finding the necessary accommodations for ourselves and our horses, we observed the remainder of the day, as a season of rest.

OSAGE CAPTIVE.

CHAPTER II.

A generous donation to redeem the Osage Captive. Difficulties in the way of obtaining her release. The author returns through the wilderness and visits the place where she lives. On account of a supposed order of Government her Indian owner declines giving her up. Application to the Osages in her behalf. Application to the Government. President directs her to be placed in the missionary school at Brainerd. She is brought to Brainerd and is named Lydia Carter.

IT will readily be imagined, that the occurrences related in the last chapter, left a deep impression upon my mind. As I pursued my journey, I felt more and more solicitous to know what would be the result of the interview at Caney-creek; and waited with some impatience to receive letters from Brainerd.

On my arrival at Natchez, the capital of the state of Mississippi, I often related the history of the Little Osage Captive. It happened upon one of these occasions, that Mrs. Lydia Carter,[2] a worth lady who lived a few miles from Natchez, was present, and heard the recital. Her heart was touched with pity; and in a few days I had the satisfaction to hear from her, that if one hundred and fifty dollars would ransom the child, she was willing to appropriate that sum for the purpose.

So unexpected and generous a donation, encouraged the hope, that she was soon to be released from captivity, and permanently placed in the missionary family at Brainerd. But in this we were disappointed. A letter received from Mr. Kingsbury, after my arrival at New Orleans, and more than two months subsequently to the transactions at Caney-creek,

---

[2] Since, Mrs. Williams of Brimfield, Mass.

informed me that the Indian, who claimed the child, had called, but without bringing her with him. It was also stated, that he had refused to give her up at all, except on the condition, of receiving a negro girl, of her size, in exchange for her. This, being a condition, with which the missionaries could never comply, it was impossible to say, how long she might continue in her present situation: besides, the disposition now shown to make a *slave* of her, was calculated to darken the prospect of her speedy deliverance.

It did not become us, however, to despond after the signal interpositions of Providence which had been witnessed in her behalf. I resolved, on my return from New Orleans, when I should have occasion to pass through the Cherokee country again, to visit the Indian with whom she lived; and to renew my endeavors to obtain her release.

Accordingly, in the spring of 1818, having received the sum which had been given to ransom her, I passed through the wilderness, and called at the place where she lived. It was a lonely hut in the woods, far from the dwellings of civilized people, and about sixty miles from Brainerd.

Unfortunately, the Indian who owned her was not at home. I saw his family, however, and among them the little captive, on whose account so much solicitude was felt. She appeared to remember me, and the moment she saw me, came running up with as much confidence, as if I had been her father. She seemed also to be quite happy in her new situation; having found a number of little playmates in the family with whom she lived. As I had no interpreter, it was impossible to communicate my wishes to her; and I was compelled to leave her, again, without being able to address her, in any more intelligible language than that of looks, and gestures, and the tones of my voice.

On the 14th of May, I arrived at Brainerd; and was happy to find there, that distinguished friend and servant of the missionary cause, Jeremiah Evarts, Esq.; who was travelling for his health, and had arrived a few days before me. The best measures which could be devised with Mr. Evarts and the missionaries, were now taken, to procure the release of the child, and to have her placed in the missionary family.

But new, and unexpected difficulties, arose. A report was put into circulation, among the Cherokees, that the President of the United States had requested all captives, taken in the war with the Osages to be given up; and it was understood, that the Indian who had possession of this little girl, did not feel himself at liberty, under these circumstances, to relinquish her to the missionaries, but was about to return her to her own nation.

Of the correctness of this report, we were unable to judge, with certainty. On some accounts, it seemed likely that it was true. It was very creditable to the Government, and agreed with their general conduct towards the Indians, to suppose, that they had thus interposed their influence in the cause of humanity. Such a step might also be viewed by them, as the most probable means of restoring peace to the tribes, and preventing the recurrence of other and still greater calamities.

Far, indeed, was it from our wishes, to do any thing to defeat this benevolent intention. But even supposing that the request had been made, it was believed that an exception might be granted in favor of the present case. The child in question, was very young; and but poorly able, to endure the hardships of another journey, of several hundred miles, through the wilderness. Both her parents were declared by the Cherokees, to be dead; and if she returned, it was to be feared there was neither kindred nor home to receive her. Why, then, might she not be left at Brainerd, where so many advantages existed for promoting her present, and future happiness? It was presumed that the Osages, themselves, would be willing to have her left there, could they be properly informed, of the wishes of those, who were desirous of giving her an education; and if they should consent, the Government would no doubt approve of the measure.

While we were thus deliberating on the subject, information was received, that a deputation of Indians, from the tribe to which she belonged was soon to meet at St. Louis, in the

Territory of Missouri, for the purpose of holding a council with his Excellency William Clark; Governor of the Territory, and Agent of the United States, for that tribe. We resolved, to take this opportunity to make known our wishes to the Osages, and if possible, to obtain their consent, to have the child left at Brainerd. In pursuance of this design, a letter was addressed by Mr. Evarts to Governor Clark,—acquainting him with the facts, and soliciting his friendly aid in accomplishing the plan which had been proposed.

No answer was received to this communication, until late in the following autumn. In the mean time, Mr. Evarts and myself, had taken leave of our friends at Brainerd, and in the hope that it might yet be called for, had committed to them the ransom money given by Mrs. Carter. Finding it convenient as we returned, to pass through Washington, we determined to lay the subject before the Government; and if the President approved the measure, to request that the child might be received into the school by his authority, and retained there during his pleasure. It was thought that this course might be taken, without giving any just cause of complaint to the Indians. It would not bind the President to any measures, which would oppose the wishes of the Osages;—at the same time, it would remove a principal objection, in the mind of the Indian who possessed the child, against giving her up, and enable the missionaries, perhaps, to ransom her without further delay.

Upon our arrival at Washington, we conversed on the subject with the Agent of Indian Trade, Thomas L. McKenney, Esq.,—whose exertions for the good of the Indians, are well known, and entitle him to the gratitude of the community. He approved of our design, and offered us all the aid in his power.

Our next interview, was with the Secretary of War, the Honorable John C. Calhoun. From him we learned that the Government had not requested the captives to be given up, as reported among the Cherokees. He received us with kindness and treated our object, with deep and friendly interest. He assured us, he would take the first opportunity to lay the subject before the President; and would inform us of the result, We soon learned that the President approved of the plan, and would take measures to carry it into effect. A letter was accordingly forwarded, by the Secretary of War, to Col. Meigs, the Agent of the United States for the Cherokee tribe, authorizing him to obtain the child and place her in the school at Brainerd.

Thus, through the humanity of the Government, whose conduct towards the Indians has, in many other instances, been such as to do them the highest honor, we had a prospect of soon gaining our object. The little girl, whose freedom has so long been sought, had become the subject of many hopes and prayers;—and God, who had so remarkably encouraged them, we doubted not, had many blessings in store for her.

On the 28th of Sept. the missionaries at Brainerd, received the joyful intelligence, that the Osage captive was within four miles of them, and would be sent to them, the first opportunity. Unwilling, however, that her arrival should be deferred another day, the Rev. Ard Hoyt, who had succeeded Mr. Kingsbury in the charge of the establishment, went immediately for her, and had the happiness to introduce her, himself, to Brainerd.

The scene which took place, in the interview, first with Mr. Hoyt and subsequently with the mission school and family—is thus described in the Brainerd Journal.

"On seeing the dear orphan, who appears to be four or five years old, he (Mr. Hoyt) directed her to be told in Cherokee, for she does not understand English, that he would be her father. She fixed her eyes with great earnestness upon him, about half a minute; and then, with a smile reached him her bonnet, as a token that she accepted the offer, and would go with him. As he took her on the horse before him, she gave him some nuts, which she had in her hand, and leaned her head on his bosom, as if she had already found a father. She was very playful and talkative, for a while, and then fell asleep, and slept most of the way to the mission house.

"When first introduced to the family, she seemed a little surprised, on seeing so many gather around her; but the children beginning to talk to her, in a language she understood, her cheerfulness immediately returned, and she appeared to be quite at home. It is said she speaks the Cherokee language well for one of her age, though it is but little more than a year since her captivity."

It was understood that if the missionaries succeeded in obtaining her, she should be named LYDIA CARTER, in remembrance of the lady who contributed so liberally for her redemption. She was, accordingly, ever afterwards called by this name. In concluding their notice of her arrival, the missionaries say; "our feelings on the reception of this exiled orphan, may be more easily conceived than described. We feel ourselves bound not only in duty, but by the feelings of our hearts, to train her as an own child."

OSAGE CAPTIVE.

CHAPTER III.

The little Osage adopted by Mr. and Mrs. Chamberlain. Gov. Clark's letter, communicating the result of the application to the Osage chiefs. Intelligence of two other Osage captives. One of them is rescued from slavery, and placed, by order of Government, in the missionary school at Brainerd.

WE have now traced the history of the Osage captive, from the time she was first met with, at Caney-creek, to the period of her arrival at Brainerd. For ten months, her case had been in a state of suspense; and it was not until much exertion had been made, that her deliverance was effected. But it was a rich reward for all the pains which had been taken, that so good a home was provided for her at last. Here, it was hoped, she would long remain, and enjoy the protection of friends, who not only loved her, but would pray for her, and instruct her in a knowledge of God, and of her Savior Jesus Christ.

All the members of the missionary family regarded her with deep interest; but to the Rev. William Chamberlain and his wife, she became an object of special endearment. To them, the immediate care of her education was committed. They received her into their family, and adopted her, as their own child. She was taught to call them father, and mother, and to feel towards them as such; while they addressed her as their daughter—and as the sister of another little daughter whom they had, whose name was Catharine.

It would be pleasant to proceed to give some account of the manner in which she spent her time with these new friends; but there are some things of an interesting nature connected with her history, which deserve to be previously mentioned.

One of them is, the result of the application, made through Governor Clark, to the Osage Chiefs, for leave to obtain her, and educate her at Brainerd. Not long after she had been placed in the school, by the authority of the President, a letter was received from Governor Clark, which gave the missionaries some uneasiness, and materially affected her future prospects. The letter was addressed to Mr. Evarts, and is as follows:—

"St. Louis, Oct. 8, 1818.
"SIR,—In compliance with the generous and humane wishes expressed in your letter of the 3rd of June last, I have made several applications to the Osages. A few days since, in a general council at this place, a formal application was made directly to the father of the child, (who was not killed in the battle as the Cherokees supposed.) He seemed much flattered at the interest, his child had excited, but would not consent to part with it, to be taken so far off. Indeed, the whole nation[3] appear to feel great repugnance at the idea of trusting their offspring in the hands of strangers, at a distance from them. They all feel the force of parental affection, but know very little of social confidence.

Signed, WILLIAM CLARK."

Many thanks were due to the Governor for the kind interest which he had shown upon this occasion. The fact that the father of the child was supposed to be still alive,—though it greatly surprised us, after all which the Cherokees had said relative to the death of *both* her parents,—was a sufficient reason why the application had failed. For, as the Governor intimates in his letter, there are no people more fond of their children, than the Indians, or more unwilling to part with them, except where they

---

[3] The word *nation* is frequently applied, by persons in the western country, to a tribe of Indians. It may appear singular, but bodies of people, so small as the Indian tribes, should be spoken of in this manner; but when we consider that they generally speak a different language, it does not appear to be a very improper use of the word.

know the individuals into whose hands they entrust them, and feel assured of seeing them again.

Whether, therefore, the Indian mentioned by Governor Clark, should prove to be the father of Lydia Carter or not,—and there were some reasons for thinking he was not,—the fact that the Osages, considered him as such, was a circumstance which could not but render her continuance at Brainerd, very doubtful. Still, the missionaries had received her into the school by the direction of the President of the United States,—and they were not at liberty to part with her except by an order from him. They felt happy in thinking that Providence had committed her to them; and would continue her under their care so long as it was best. They resolved, therefore, to proceed in educating her and training her up, as their own child: trusting in God, that he would bless their endeavors to guide her into the way of eternal life. Her adopted parents, having formed these views, dedicated her to God, in the ordinance of baptism, on the 10th of January 1819.

We are now to relate another interposition of Providence, scarcely less remarkable than that which occurred in the deliverance of the child, to whose history we have been attending.

On the first of December 1818, Col. Meigs, the venerable and worthy Agent before mentioned, informed the missionaries at Brainerd, that a Cherokee, residing in a distant part of the tribe, had an Osage boy in his possession, who was taken at the same time with Lydia Carter; and, that, as he was about to return to the Arkansaw country, he would leave the boy with them, provided they would go after him. Information was also received, that the same Indian had in his family an Osage girl, who was said to be Lydia's sister.

Upon receiving this intelligence, Mr. Hoyt and one of his sons, set out in pursuit of the children, hoping to obtain them both. They were gone nine days; during which time, they travelled between two and three hundred miles, and were obliged to lie out in the woods several nights, and to suffer various other hardships. They saw both the children, but were unable to obtain either of them. The girl was, indeed, Lydia Carter's sister; and appeared to be about 15 years of age. The boy was not more than four or five years old. Mr. Hoyt did all he could to procure their release; but the Indian with whom they lived refused to give them up, and said that the Agent had misunderstood him.

Nothing more was heard concerning them for several months. All supposed that they had accompanied their owner to the Arkansaw country, and were far removed from the light of civilization and Christianity. But in August of the ensuing year, the missionaries were told that the Cherokee with whom they lived, had not removed, as was expected, to the Arkansaw country, and that probably he would not remove there at all. They also learned, that he had sold the boy to a white man, who had moved into the tribe, and was living there as an intruder. It happened not long after, that Mr. Chamberlain, the adopted father of Lydia Carter, had occasion to travel near the place where the man lived. He did not see the boy, but ascertained that he had been sold for the trifling sum of twenty dollars. In a few weeks, information was communicated, that he had been sold again, to another white man, for one hundred and fifty dollars.

It was now evident that a plan was laid to enslave the defenceless child; and no time was to be lost in preventing the cruel design from being effected. The missionaries conferred with their friends on the subject, and Mr. John Ross, a respectable young man living in the neighborhood of Brainerd, offered to go in pursuit of the boy, and to rescue him. That he might be more certain of gaining his object, application was made by Mr. Ross to Col. Meigs, for authority to take him wherever he might be found, and bring him to Brainerd. The Agent, acting in the name of the President of the United States, issued an order accordingly; and Mr. Ross, with two assistants, set out on the 27th of September. When he commenced the journey, he was unable to tell certainly, where the child was; but at length, at the distance of 250 miles from Brainerd, he found him. On coming near to the place, it is stated by the missionaries in their journal, that, "he took the precaution to leave his horses behind him, and approached silently on foot. He found the boy entirely naked, in the yard before the house, and took him in his arms before he made his business known to the family. The man disclaimed all intentions of keeping the boy in slavery, and wished Mr. Ross to leave him a short time, until they could prepare him some clothes. But he refused to leave him a moment, or to suffer him to sleep from him a night."

From the neighbors, it is further stated in the journal, Mr. Ross learned, that the man had said the boy was a mullatto, born in slavery;—and that he intended, in a few days, to take him to market and sell him. He was also informed that the same man had endeavored to persuade another person to join him in this horrid traffic; telling him that there were a number of captives in the Cherokee nation, whom he thought he could obtain at a low price.

By this timely and disinterested effort, another captive was obtained, and saved from a state of hopeless bondage. After an absence of thirteen days, during which time he travelled six hundred miles, Mr. Ross returned to Brainerd, and had the pleasure of committing the boy to the kind and faithful guardianship of the missionary family. He appeared to be much delighted with his new situation. He had forgotten his native tongue, but having been much with the white people, he could speak English with considerable fluency. Although he was very young,—being even smaller than Lydia Carter, he discovered many traits of an active and sprightly mind. On being told by some one, that he would find a father and mother at Brainerd— he answered with quickness and animation, "Yes, and *bread too*."

By the missionaries he was named John Osage Ross, in honor of his kind deliverer. He was adopted by Mr. Hoyt, as Lydia had been by Mr. Chamberlain, and was given to God in baptism on the 12th of December 1819. In January following, notice was communicated by the Agent, that the Government approved of what had been done, and that the child could not be removed from the missionary school but by the authority of the President.

Thus, by a number of remarkable Providences, two little captives, belonging to the same tribe of Indians, were rescued, and placed in an institution which afforded them every advantage for improvement. Another was still in bondage: but whether it would be possible to obtain her and place her in the same institution with her ransomed sister, could not be determined.

CHAPTER IV.

Situation and appearance of Brainerd. Its buildings; cultivated fields; and grave-yard. Design of the institution. Plan of instruction. Its advantages above other plans of instructing the Indians. Its success. Death of Dr. Worcester.

As the institution in which Lydia Carter was placed, is one which has excited deep interest among all the friends of the missionary cause, it will be expected, perhaps, by my young readers, that I should give some account of it.

It was begun by Mr. Kingsbury, who has before been mentioned, in January, 1817. He had been sent out as a missionary to the Cherokee Indians, by the American Board of Commissioners for Foreign Missions. At the time he selected this spot for the seat of the mission, there belonged to it a few acres only of cleared ground, and three or four log cabins which were occupied by a white man who had married an Indian wife. These, Mr. Kingsbury purchased; and without any assistant began to make preparation for an establishment which has since grown up into one of great importance. In May 1818, it received the name of Brainerd; in memory of David Brainerd, the excellent missionary, whose labors were so much blessed among the Indians in New Jersey, about eighty years ago.

The place where the institution stands, is two miles north of the line which divides the state of Georgia from the state of Tennessee, on the south west side of a small river, called Chick-a-mau-gáh creek. On approaching it from the north east, you come to the creek at the distance of fifty rods from the principal mission house. Immediately you leave the woods, and crossing the stream, which is from four to six rods wide, you enter an area of cleared ground, on the right of which, appear numerous buildings of various kinds and sizes. At the distance of a few steps, stand a grist mill and saw mill, turned by a canal three quarters of a mile in length, which conducts the water from a branch of the creek in the neighborhood. A little further, you come to a lane, on either side of which, are several houses occupied by laborers and mechanics, of various descriptions. Following the lane, which runs across the cleared ground, you pass a large and commodious barn, with some other buildings, and are conducted directly in front of a row of houses, which forms the principal part of the settlement, and makes a prominent appearance in the view of Brainerd.

Nearly in the centre of the row, is the mission house, two stories high, having a piazza its whole length, with a pleasant court yard in front of it. It is occupied by the superintendant and other missionaries. Behind it, and immediately connected with it, is the dining hall and kitchen for the establishment. On your right, and at the distance of a few feet, stands another building of two stories, which is used for the instruction of girls. It is well finished, and was built by the particular direction of the President of the United States, who called here in 1819, on his tour through the western states. Many smaller buildings are ranged upon the right and left of these two, and afford convenient lodging places for the children, and other persons, connected with the institution.

Passing onward, about thirty rods, to the end of the lane which has been mentioned, you come to the school house for the boys; which stands in the edge of the woods, and is large enough to accommodate one hundred scholars. On the Sabbath it is used also as a place of worship. The whole number of buildings belonging to the institution, exceeds thirty. They are, most of them, however, constructed of logs, and make but a plain appearance.

The ground, on the south east side of the lane,[4] is divided into a garden, an orchard, and several other lots, which are

---

[4] The direction of the lane is north east and south west.

OSAGE CAPTIVE.

VIEW OF BRAINERD.

A – *Dr. Worcester's Grave*

Boston, S. T. Armstrong & Crocker & Brewster.   New York, John P. Haven.

neatly fenced in, and present a pleasant prospect in front of the mission house. In a corner of the orchard, next the school house, is the grave yard; where lie the bodies of those who have died at the institution, and among them the remains of that great and good man, the Rev. Dr. Worcester; who having worn out his life in the service of Christ and the heathen, ended his days at this place on the 7th of June, 1821.

The whole circumference of ground which has been described may not, perhaps, include fifty acres; but being in the midst of a wilderness, whose deep forests appear on every side, it presents to the beholder a scene of cultivation and of active and cheerful life, which cannot but inspire him with pleasure. To the Christian, who contemplates the moral wilderness by which it is surrounded, it presents a prospect more delightful than tongue can express.

The design of the institution is to instruct the natives in the Gospel; and to teach them the most necessary arts of civilized life. These ends are not pursued separately; but are carried on together. In this respect, the plan of the institution differs from almost all former missions to the Indians. For while one class of Christians have maintained that the first thing to be done, was to civilize the Indians, and then convert them to christianity; another class have contended that it was necessary, first to convert them, and that then they would become civilized of course. It was conceived by those who formed the plan of the Brainerd institution, that both these objects are so closely connected, they may be pursued at the same time.

To a person, therefore, who visits Brainerd, the settlement appears like that of a numerous christian family; the members of which are employed in the various duties of civilized and christian life. Some are occupied in the field—some in the workshop—and some in the domestic cares of the family. The children of the Indians who are brought here for instruction, are provided with schools according to their sex, and taught the most useful branches in human and divine knowledge. When they are out of school, a part of their time is spent in relaxation, and a part in labor. The boys are taken to the farm, and taught the arts of husbandry; or to the shop of the mechanic, where they are instructed in some useful trade: while the girls learn to spin and to weave, to knit and to sew, or take their turns in waiting upon the table, or serving in the kitchen. When the hour for devotion comes, all are assembled to offer unto God the sacrifice of morning or evening prayer. On the Sabbath, they repair to the house of worship, and unite in its solemn services. The Gospel is preached not only to those who belong to the institution, but to as many of the natives, from the surrounding country, as can be induced to attend. The congregation assembled upon these occasions is not large, but one of the most interesting which a minister ever addresses. For besides the missionaries, and teachers, and christian laborers, who with their families attend— he beholds seated before him, from eighty to one hundred Indian children, who are taught in the English language, and are growing up in all the habits of a civilized and christian people. Some of them have already made considerable progress in their education, and, in the judgment of charity, have been truly converted to God. Assembled with them, are many of their Indian parents and friends, who listen with fixed and silent attention to what the preacher is saying, and not unfrequently drop the tear of sincere and lively interest, while he opens to them the word of God, and shows them the way of salvation.

These things, the writer states, not from information merely, but from what his own eyes have seen, and his ears heard, while sojourning a few weeks at this delightful spot. He has seen an Indian warrior who was famed for his courage, melt into tenderness, on hearing the love and mercy of God through Jesus Christ described; and he has known him, the day after, to come several miles that he might disclose the burden on his mind, and ask the missionaries the plain and solemn question:—"Can you tell me what God wants me to do?" And he has seen this same warrior, humbly sitting at the feet of Jesus, and rejoicing in him, as his all-sufficient Savior. The habits and feelings of the savage were no longer perceived: they were exchanged for those of the industrious man, and consistent Christian.

Nor have these proofs of the presence and blessing of God, been seldom witnessed. Numbers of the natives, and others who reside in the vicinity of Brainerd, have been induced to renounce their sins, and embrace the religion of Christ. Some of them have been ornaments to the church. Of the children and youth, who have been instructed here, and given evidence of piety, several have already been the means of much good to their acquaintance and friends; and promise to be yet more extensively useful to their tribe. Thus, while one of them is instructing a school of Indian children, at the distance of one hundred miles from Brainerd, where she has already witnessed the conversion of her parents, and of some of her other relatives:—another, who is her brother, is pursuing his studies in the missionary school at Cornwall, in Connecticut, and qualifying himself to preach the Gospel to his ignorant countrymen. Several other youths, whose course of instruction was begun at Brainerd, are expected to become missionaries and teachers in their native tribe. Some idea of their attainments, and of the prospects they give of future usefulness, may be obtained from a few of their letters published in the Appendix.

But the good which this institution has done, is not confined to those who have been immediately connected with it. It has proved to the world, that the Indians may be civilized, and converted to Christianity. Thousands, who before doubted whether this could be done, doubt it no longer. A general interest has been awakened for the Indians; and multitudes are endeavoring to promote their temporal and eternal happiness. Other causes have undoubtedly had an influence to bring about this result; but they have begun to operate chiefly, since Mr. Kingsbury commenced his labors at Brainerd.

A place like this, then, will ever be strongly endeared to the hearts of christians. Here, it was, that the long night of Indian darkness began to disperse. Other attempts had been made to do good to the natives, which had cast some light over their prospects; but, nothing had been done, which seemed so much like the dawn of an approaching day. Here, also, it was, that the man, whose wise and faithful counsels had contributed so much to establish and build up the institution, was called, by a mysterious Providence, to die. Scarcely, had he time to witness the success of his labors, and to behold the answer to his prayers, when his spirit fled to receive its reward in heaven. At this consecrated spot, his body is fast mouldering into dust:—but while the name of WORCESTER is revered and loved, that dust will be remembered, and Brainerd, with whose soil it has mingled, will not be forgotten.

CHAPTER V.

Character and conduct of Lydia Carter while at Brainerd. Progress in learning. Her religious feelings. Affection for her adopted parents and friends. Her gratitude to her benefactors. Recollection of her Osage parents. The manner of her mother's death.

SUCH was the institution, to which little Lydia Carter, was brought. The advantages which it afforded her, for improvement, were great. If, in addition to this, we consider that Mr. and Mrs. Chamberlain had adopted her, as their own child, and, that they ever after, treated her with the care and affection, of the tenderest parents; it may well be doubted, whether there are many children, even in christian lands, whose situation is happier, than was hers. The manner, in which she conducted, while at Brainerd, and the progress she made in her education, next claims our attention.

When she arrived at the institution, the missionaries supposed that she might be about five years of age. She had no knowledge of the English language; but so rapidly did she acquire it, that in less than a year, from the time she entered the school, she was able to speak it, as well as children commonly do, who have learned no other language.

In a letter, recently received from Mr. Chamberlain, he says: "She discovered a very strong mind for one of her age. She was apt to learn; but owing to hardships, which she experienced before she arrived here, she was sick most of the time while with us, which retarded her considerably in her education."

It will be recollected, that it was ten months after she was met with at Caney-creek before she was brought to Brainerd;— and judging, from some facts, which have since been disclosed,

OSAGE CAPTIVE.

it is probable that she had been taken captive, two months before. So that when she fell into the hands of the Cherokees, she could not have been older, than four years. This, was a tender period of life, to undertake such a journey through the wilderness, as she had to perform. Nor will it appear strange, that it should have injured her health, for a long time after, when we consider, that she travelled eight hundred miles, at a most unpleasant season of the year, and through a country, which afforded only a scanty supply of food.

Notwithstanding her health was so poor, she still made considerable progress in learning. She could read in easy lessons, and recite a number of hymns, beside giving answers to questions in the catechism. The hymns, she had learned to sing, as well as to repeat.

Her mind was early instructed in the things of religion: and, although she gave no decisive evidence of possessing a new heart, her feelings were so serious and tender, that it seemed as if the Divine Spirit had begun to operate upon her mind. Mr. Chamberlain, speaking of her character in this respect, says:— "when Lydia first began to speak our language, and hear something about God, she would sometimes be almost lost in thought; and would frequently show the depth of her mind, by her pertinent questions. When her mother told her, that God made her, she mentioned over several other things, and wanted to know, if God made them also. On being answered in the affirmative, she wanted to know what God was,—where he lived,—and who made him. She never appeared satisfied, until she understood what was told her. She frequently asked respecting things of another world; and what would become of people when they die." It is added; "she was particular, to say her prayers morning and evening."

In her feelings, she was remarkably *affectionate*, and *kind.* "I think I never saw a child," says Mr. Chamberlain, "who more fond of its parents, than she was of hers." She was unwilling to stay from them, even for a night. And nothing could be more painful to her, than the idea that she might, one day, have to leave them to return to her own tribe. The same affection, was exhibited by her towards her little sister Catharine Chamberlain; whom she greatly loved, though she was much younger than herself.

To her parents, and superiors, she was *obedient*, and *respectful*, as well as affectionate. She would sometimes do things which were wrong, but, it was not with a stubborn and wilful opposition to duty; when she had acted improperly, she would confess her faults, and appear to be sorry for them.

She was very *grateful*, for the favors which she had received, both before and after her arrival at Brainerd; and she would often speak, in the tenderest manner, of those who had been instrumental of her deliverance from captivity. The following anecdote, related by Mr. Chamberlain, in one of his letters, illustrates this trait in her character, so strikingly, that the writer hopes he shall be pardoned for inserting it; notwithstanding, it refers to himself. The letter, was written a little more than a year, after her arrival at Brainerd. In it Mr. Chamberlain says; "Lydia Carter appears to be a promising child. She often speaks of you, and considers you, as her deliverer. She was very much disappointed a few days ago:— she was out in the yard, and saw a person ride up, whom she fancied to be Mr. Cornelius. She ran in, with great haste, and cried out, Mother, mother, Mr. Cornelius is come. But the poor child was soon undeceived, and hung her head."

In the midst of so many other friends, she still remembered her Osage parents; and she would sometimes speak of the calamity which separated her from them. Of the fate of her father, nothing was certainly known; but in respect of her mother, it was very different. Her death, had made an impression upon her mind too deep, ever to be forgotten. "At one time," says Mr. Chamberlain, "she related to me the circumstances of her mother being killed. She said, as they were sitting in the bushes, some men came and shot her mother in the breast, and the blood ran along upon the ground. The men came then, and took her, and put her on a horse, and she fell off. She said, one time on her way here, she rode along through a creek, and the water came up all around her." In confirmation of this statement, Mr. Chamberlain says; "as near as I can learn these things were true."

It is delightful to think, how Providence had relieved her from all these misfortunes, by placing her at Brainerd. Here, she found a home, dearer to her than any she had enjoyed before; and parents were raised up, who had it in their power to do far more to promote her happiness, than those whom she had lost.

CHAPTER VI.

Intelligence received at Brainerd that the Osages had demanded the captives; and that an authorized Agent had come to receive them. Intelligence confirmed, and the Agent arrives at Brainerd with orders from Colonel Meigs. Distress occasioned by this event. The captives given up. Parting scene.

GREAT hopes were entertained, that the interesting child, whose character and conduct have been described, and the little boy, who had been taken with her, would be allowed to remain, and grow up, under the care of those excellent friends, who had adopted them as their children. But God, who sees things, not as man sees them, had otherwise determined.

Ever since the arrival of Lydia Carter, and, especially, after Governor Clark's letter had been received, the missionaries had felt some apprehension, that the Osages would demand her in a formal manner, and that the President, by whose direction she had been left at Brainerd, would, feel himself obliged to grant their request. Two years had nearly past, and the strongest attachment had been formed between her, and her adopted connexions; when news came that the demand had been made, and that she must soon be taken from them.

The pain, which this intelligence gave, both to the parents and the child, may be learned from the following extract of a letter, written by Mr. Chamberlain, at the time. It is dated, August 4, 1820. "My wife and myself are in trouble at present, and wish your prayers. We expect every day, to lose our dear Osage daughter. There has a man come from the Arkansaw, for her and the other captives. Brother Hicks[5] thinks they will be

---

[5] Mr. Hicks is a half-blood Cherokee, the second beloved man, or chief of the tribe, and a member of the Moravian church at Spring Place.

obliged to go. I know they cannot take Lydia, without orders from the President; but the man is waiting at the Agency, probably for orders. We have not dared to tell her, what the prospects are; though she got some hint of it among the children the other day. She ran to her mother in great surprise, and said, 'Mother, they say some people have come after me,—but mother wont let me go, will she?' Her mother could not answer her, and it passed off. It will no doubt be as hard for her to leave us, as for any other child, of her age, to leave its parents; and I think it will be as hard for us to part with her, as though she were our own. But the Lord will direct."

In this state of suspense, every thing remained, until the 22d of August. On that day, a person, commissioned by government, arrived at Brainerd, with orders to take Lydia Carter and John Osage Ross. The letter, addressed by Colonel Meigs, to the missionaries, upon this trying occasion states, that Governor Miller, of the territory of Arkansaw, had been authorized by the Government of the United States, to settle a difficulty between the Arkansaw Cherokees and the Osages, who were on the point of engaging in another destructive war;—that the Governor had met the parties, and brought them to suspend hostilities, on condition that the Cherokees should return the captives whom they had taken, and that the Osages should give up certain men, who had murdered three of the Cherokees;—that these conditions, having been solemnly agreed to, on both sides, the Government felt it their duty to compel the parties to fulfil them; and, finally, that Governor Miller, acting in behalf of the United States, now demanded the delivery of the prisoners, on one side; and of the murderers, on the other.

Colonel Meigs remarks in the letter, that Governor Miller had assured him, he would use his influence to have the children returned to Brainerd again; and then adds—"I am sensible it must be painful to you to part with them; but, it seems the only measure to be adopted, to prevent the shedding of much blood. Mr. John Rogers, a kind and humane man, will take the best possible care of them. I request that the children may be comfortably furnished, with every thing necessary and proper for their journey, and I will pay your bills for the same. * * * * * I request you, to deliver the two little prisoners, to Mr. Rogers. I am confident, that he will be governed by your advice, and will, in every respect act towards them kindly, and tenderly."

The effect which this communication produced, cannot be better described, than by quoting the journal of the missionaries.

"This message," say they, "was inexpressibly distressing, to all the mission family; especially, to those who had adopted these children, as their own. We had, some days since, been informed that the children were demanded, and had reason to expect they must be given up; but still, were not without hope, that by some means they might yet be retained, till they should be prepared to carry the knowledge of the Savior to their people. All hope is now taken away. They must be given up: not to the arms of death, but to a call from the wilderness; to be taken back, probably, to a savage life. We can only commend them to the care of that gracious Redeemer, to whom they have been devoted in baptism, and who is still able to preserve, and bring them, where they can receive that instruction, which we would gladly have given, and by means of which they may still be prepared for usefulness in life, peace in death, and happiness beyond the grave."

The journal next states the effect, which the communication had on the children.

"John Osage Ross, being younger, and not having been so long with us, was not much affected. But Lydia Carter, had become strongly attached to us all; especially, to brother and sister Chamberlain, whom she called father and mother. She knew no other parents; consequently, the thought of a separation, was peculiarly trying to her, as well as to us.

"When she heard that Mr. Rogers had come for her, which was early in the morning, she, in company with another little girl, escaped to the woods. All the persons about the house, including the children of the school, went in pursuit of her, but without success. A little after noon, one of our neighbors came and informed us, that he had seen them about three miles from this place, on their way to the girl's father. Milo Hoyt, was immediately sent to fetch Lydia. When he came to the house of the little girl's father, he learned that Lydia had been there, but fearing some one would know where she was, and come for her, she could not rest contented until she went two miles further; making in all, *five miles*, which she travelled through the woods to avoid being taken.

"When she first saw Milo, she appeared somewhat frightened, and began to cry; but he soon consoled her, by telling her some pleasing things, about the man who had come for her, and what she would see on the way. On returning, she appeared cheerful; and learning that we thought it best for her to go, she said she was willing. This relieved our feelings very much; as we could never before make her consent to go away on any terms; and we feared, she would have been forced from us. She remained very cheerful, and sung in our family worship with her usual animation."

The following morning, was the time fixed upon for her departure. Having a trunk, and some other articles, which it was inconvenient to carry, she desired her mother to keep them; and, in case she should never return, to give them to her sister Catharine:—adding pleasantly, 'Here is a little handkerchief, too small for me; I wish you to give this to Catharine, whether I come back or not.' "

In describing the final separation, the journal says: "She remained composed till just before they started; and, then, appeared in deep thought. She looked around on those she loved, for the last time, and then dropped her head, and the tears flowed profusely. She walked out to the horse, without being bidden; and, notwithstanding her evident grief, she was not heard to sob aloud, except when taking leave of her little sister Catharine. Her whole appearance through this trying scene, was like that of a person of mature age, in like circumstances. It is the Lord; let him do what seemeth him good.

"Little John, having been told from the beginning, that if he would go willingly, without crying, he would have the horse on which he was to ride, and the saddle and the bridle for his own; went off smiling, and was apparently much pleased with his newly acquired property."

The journal in concluding this affecting account, expresses the hope, that the children on their return to the Osage country, would be taken into the missionary school at Union, which had been established a short time before by the United Foreign Mission Society. But God had other purposes in view, which as they respected Lydia Carter, were soon to be accomplished.

OSAGE CAPTIVE.

CHAPTER VII.

The Captives, a few days after their departure arrive at Creek-Path. The happiness of Lydia Carter on seeing some of her Brainerd friends. She pursues her journey and is taken to Governor Miller. Governor Miller takes her with the other Captives to the Osage country. She and little John are given back to the Governor. Lydia returns with him as far as the country of the Arkansaw Cherokees, and is left at the house of a white woman. Her health having long been poor—she is taken sick and dies. Conclusion.

IT was on the twenty-third of August, 1820, that the captives left Brainerd. The weather was very warm, and a long journey was before them. After travelling a hundred miles they came to a settlement in the western part of the Cherokee nation, called Creek-Path. It is situated on the south side of the Tennessee river, about thirty miles from Huntsville, in the state of Alabama. The place is interesting on account of its being the residence of the parents, and some other relatives of Catharine Brown, who was one of the earliest converts in the school at Brainerd. Catharine had returned to Creek-Path when Lydia arrived, and was instructing a school of Indian girls. Some of her other Brainerd acquaintance were there also, who were engaged in making preparations for a new missionary establishment.

Her feelings, on meeting these kind and sympathizing friends may easily be imagined. They served to renew for a while the pleasure which she had lost. One of Mr. Hoyt's daughters happened to be there at the time, and returned not long after to Brainerd. The missionaries, speaking of some intelligence received by her, state the following circumstances in their journal: "She also informs that she saw our dear little Lydia, on her way to the Osages. Lydia told her, she wished she could write to her father and mother. Sister A. told her, she would write for her, if she could tell what she wanted to say. She appeared pleased with this, and began, and was able to say only a few words, before she was so much affected that she could not proceed. She said she wanted her father and mother to come to the Osage country and take her."

The particulars of her journey from this place have not been received. We learn, however that she was taken to Governor Miller in the course of the autumn, and that by him, she was conducted, with the other captives, to the Osage tribe, the next winter.

And here in order to give a better idea of her wanderings, it may be necessary to add something further respecting the geography of the country.

The river from which it takes its name, is one of the largest which empties into the Mississippi from the west. It is said to be more than two thousand miles long, and is navigable almost to its source. The country through which Lydia Carter travelled, lies on the north side of the river, and may be divided into three parts. First, the Territory of Arkansaw, or more properly that division of it which is inhabited by white people. Second, the country ceded by the United States to the Cherokee Indians. Third, the country belonging to the Osages.

The principal settlements of white people upon the Arkansaw river, are at the Post of Arkansaw, Little Rock, and Cadron; the former of which is sixty, and the latter four hundred miles from the mouth of the river, reckoning its various windings. The Cherokee settlement is, perhaps, one hundred miles further. Not far from it, on the west side of what is called Illinois-creek, and five miles above its junction with the Arkansaw, stands DWIGHT. This is a missionary establishment, begun by the American Board in 1820, and named in honor of the late President Dwight, who was a distinguished member of the Board, and a zealous friend of missions. The great Osage village, near which the Union Institution is seated, is two hundred and fifty miles still further west. The whole distance from the mouth of the Arkansaw river to the Osage village is nine hundred miles;—across the country in a straight line it may be two or three hundred miles less.

Over this whole extent of country Lydia Carter had once before travelled, and was now to pass it again. Being under the protection of Governor Miller, she with the other captives left Little Rock, early in 1821, and ascended the river to the Osage country. The Governor hoped that by restoring them to the Osages himself, he could more easily persuade them to fulfil the stipulations which were made on their part the year before, and thus put an end to the contest between them and the Cherokees. But when he arrived, he found the whole tribe bent upon war, and neither his solicitations nor their own engagements could induce them to give up the murderers.

What became of the other children is not known. But Lydia Carter and John Osage Ross, having been restored to their tribe, or as the Osages termed it, "having been raised from the dead"— were given back to the Governor, by his request. Lydia was to be returned to her parents and friends at Brainerd by the first opportunity, and John was to live with the Governor and accompany him on a journey which he was soon to make to New England. The Osages particularly requested that he would take the boy to Washington, and "show him to their great father, the President."[6] Who they saw on their arrival, or whether their parents were still living is not known. It seems probable, from the fact that they were so readily given back to the Governor, that their nearest relations were not there to retain them.

On the Governor's return, he took them with him; and Lydia rejoiced to think that a few months more of wearisome journeying would bring her to her dear friends at Brainerd. But her wanderings were to be ended long before she had crossed the wilderness which lay between them. God, who has promised

---

[6] It is understood that little John was taken to Washington for this purpose. He has since returned to the Arkansaw country, and if we are correctly informed, is living with Governor Miller.

that he will be a Father of the fatherless, had provided for her, it is hoped, a better home; and he was about to remove her thither.

From the time she entered the Arkansaw country her health was poor. In consequence of frequent and long exposures to the weather she was seized with the fever and ague, and was never entirely well afterwards. When the Governor returned with her from the Osage country, he thought her too feeble to proceed on her journey, and concluded to leave her with the missionaries at Dwight, until she should be better, and a favorable opportunity should occur for sending her to Brainerd.

Several of the missionaries being absent, and no female having yet arrived at the establishment, she was placed under the care of Mrs. Lovely, a kind and hospitable white woman, who is the widow of a former Agent of the United States, and lives about a day's ride from Dwight. At what time, she arrived here has not been ascertained, but it was probably in the month of March.

It is said that she had no attack of fever and ague, after she came to Mrs. Lovely's; but appeared to have been worn out by exposures while she was weak. Her strength failed rapidly; and death was evidently near. But her mind was calm, and a sweet resignation to the will of God was shown by her, through all her sickness. She frequently repeated the hymns which she had learned at Brainerd, and seemed to derive comfort from them. They no doubt led her to think much of that Savior who died for her, and whom she promised her parents, when she left them, that "she would always remember."

In this state she continued for a few weeks, and then expired!—He, who said, "Suffer little children to come unto me and forbid them not," received her, we trust, to dwell with him for ever.

May those who read her history, remember the means by which her last moments were rendered so peaceful and happy. It was through the instrumentality of CHRISTIAN MISSIONARIES, who were sent to the Indians, to teach them the Gospel, and to show them the way of salvation, that her mind was prepared for death. Had there been no missionaries to instruct her, she had died without a knowledge of the Savior, or any of those consolations which cheered and supported her in the departing hour.

Millions of others, in Heathen lands, are still ignorant of the same Savior! What numbers of them will die before the news of his salvation can reach them! Who would not labor to save them from their wretchedness, and cheerfully deny himself of the gratifications of this life, for the sake of sending them the Gospel. Let all who enjoy its blessings, remember that God has made it their duty to communicate them to the destitute. Let children and youth consider, that they are required to do something to send the Gospel to the Heathen. How many of them might give to this object a penny a week or a penny a month, by abstaining from some unnecessary indulgence. Were all the children in our country to do this, they would raise several hundred thousand dollars every year; and their donations alone, would be sufficient to send instruction to every Indian child in America. Should the children throughout Christian lands do it, it would go far towards educating all the Heathen children in the world. May the youth who read this narrative be persuaded to embrace the Gospel themselves, and do what they can to send it to others:—and may they live to see the time fully come, when the wilderness and the solitary place shall be glad, and the desert shall rejoice; and the earth shall be full of the knowledge of the Lord, as the waters cover the sea.

LINES

COMPOSED BY A LADY ON THE DEATH OF THE LITTLE OSAGE CAPTIVE.

"If the Son make you free, ye shall be free indeed."
                                      JOHN viii, 36.

WHERE the tall forests' sable plume
  Deep shadows o'er the valley spread,
And where the cloud of Heathen gloom
  Made nature's solitude more dread,—

Consoled by no enlight'ning word,
  Bereft of counsellor and guide,
In sadness, like some prison'd bird,
  The lonely Osage orphan sigh'd.

But Christian sympathy, her woes
  Beheld, while Zeal a tribute gave,
And pure Benevolence arose
  Like Him who came the lost to save.

Borne kindly to a refuge blest,
  Where no oppressive foes intrude;
The ransom'd Captive's joyous breast,
  Became the seat of gratitude.

Encircled by a holy band
  Who shed o'er darken'd minds the day,
Humbly she rais'd the imploring hand,
  And sought to brighter worlds the way.

Made free by Jesus,—o'er the chains
  Of cold mortality she sprung,
To range in bliss the heav'nly plains,
  And praise Him with an angel's tongue.

APPENDIX.

For the gratification of my readers I subjoin the following specimens of Indian composition, nearly all of which are extracts from letters received by myself, and are now published for the first time. From these, it will be seen that the natives are not only capable of improvement, but that they are, to a high degree, desirous of possessing the means of instruction. The extracts are, from letters of Indian youth; from a correspondence with a converted Cherokee chief; and from a correspondence with a Choctaw chief. No alterations have been made except in the punctuation, and in one or two words which appeared to have been used improperly through inadvertence.

I.

EXTRACTS FROM THE LETTERS OF INDIAN YOUTH.

Nos. 1 and 2 were written by a Cherokee youth in the Foreign Mission School at Cornwall, in reply to some inquiries addressed to him respecting Lydia Carter, whom he knew at Brainerd, and at whose capture by the Arkansaw Cherokees, he was present. They will be read with interest on account of the testimony they bear to Lydia's character; and the history they give of the war in which she was taken. The writer is 18 or 20 years of age; and has been at school about 3 years. The first letter is dated Jan. 4, 1822.

"Dear Sir,
"My knowledge of the little Osage captive does not extend far, though I was one of the warriors, that traversed the Osage nation in pursuit of blood, and was present at the Osage

APPENDIX.

vanquishment, by the Cherokees, and where Lydia Carter was taken.

"To particularize the circumstances from her first capture to the time of her reception at Brainerd, I presume is not essential, as you are much acquainted with them yourself. I could not but be interested in her case when I saw her at Brainerd. She spoke the Cherokee language with a good degree of fluency considering her age. The Rev. Mr. Chamberlain kept her in his family, and I think loved her with paternal affection; therefore she called him, Pa, and Mrs. Chamberlain, Ma, and was truly a lovely daughter to them. The English language, she acquired, in some degree, in a short time. Her devoted parents early led her tender mind to the subject of religion, and she was able to rehearse a few of the most important answers in the catechism. Lydia considered little Catharine Chamberlain as her own sister, and was very fond of her.

"In fine, the dear girl was promising, amiable, dutiful to her superiors, and the prospect of her future usefulness among her kindred was truly flattering. I lamented much when I heard of her death, and remembered her poor wandering people, that are yet walking in the shades of midnight darkness. But the Lord will provide. I trust that the Board will not be discouraged in their grand enterprise of evangelizing the heathen, wherein they are so ardently engaged.

"The missionary spirit, which is now so prevalent in this land, is, I trust, from above. I pray, that the benign auspices of heaven, may still attend the American Board, and that the long degraded Indians, whose minds have been held in bondage, by the god of this world, may be brought into the fold of Christ.

"The anticipation is truly animating when the gospel of the kingdom, shall be preached to every soul in America, and when righteousness and peace shall reign to the Pacific Ocean."

The other letter referred to, was written Jan. 17, 1822, in answer to further inquiries on the same subject. It opens with an account of the origin of the war between the Osages and Cherokees.

APPENDIX.

"Revenge you know, is one of the characteristics of an Indian, and that was the principle cause of the war between the Cherokees and Osages. This war had been carried on for many years, and in its commencement I think was occasioned by a few hunters of both nations, being on the same ground, and taking from each other peltry and fur, till they began to slay each other. I wish here to be understood correctly. The above hunters, were not the leading men in each tribe, by any means; but wild and bloody men that regarded not the interest of their countrymen, and so were the two nations obliged to unbury the tomahawk of war. The engagement took place 30 or 40 miles west of the Osage village, and I presume 200 from the Cadron, which is 30 miles from the Dardanelles.[1] There were 600 of the Cherokees and their allies, the Shawnees, and Delawares. As to the number of combatant Osages I do not know; perhaps they were not so numerous as their enemies; and they did not stand to fight, except a small company, who were immediately conquered. They fled from their encampments, men, women, and children, to the mountains and vales. Sixty souls were the number taken, and killed, including women and children, and little Lydia was one of the prisoners that were taken. The Shawnees took some captives to their own country. I do not know what became of Lydia's parents, it is difficult to determine, as there was much bustle at the time, and I heard nothing on the subject afterwards. All the captives were taken at the same time. The expedition was in the year 1817, and I think, in the month of October. General Ta-lon-tis-kee[2] was at the head of the Cherokee army. Every warrior (among Indians) is entitled to as many captives, as he can take, and may dispose of them as he pleases, and it was thus with the man that took Lydia.

"Should this communication answer your wishes, I shall feel happy. And may the Lord our Savior bless you, in your useful enterprises is the prayer of your unworthy friend."

---

[1] The place of the Cherokee settlement on the Arkansaw river.

[2] A Cherokee Indian, of unusual enterprize, who is since dead.

APPENDIX.

No. 3. Copy of a letter from a female convert in the school at Brainerd, written in Jan. 1820, after she had been at school two years and a half. It is addressed to a lady in New England who had opened a correspondence with her, and who in a letter to the present publisher says, "The hand writing of the epistle is good, its orthography correct, and the composition precisely as follows:"

"DEAR SISTER IN CHRIST,

"I thank you much for your affectionate letter, which I received on the 23d of December. O, how great, how rich is the mercy of our dear Redeemer! who has made us the subjects of his kingdom, and led us, as we trust from death unto life. My dear sister, I can never express my gratitude to God, for his goodness towards me, and my dear people. Surely it is of *his own glorious mercy*, that he is sending to us the Gospel of the Lord Jesus, in this distant land, where the people had long set in darkness, and were perishing for lack of the knowledge of God. Blessed be his holy name! O my sister let us rejoice continually in our Lord and Savior, and as we have put on Christ, not only by outward profession, but by inward and spiritual union, let us walk worthy of our high and holy vocation, and shew the world, that there is something in true religion. And may the Lord give us strength to do his will, and to follow continually the example of our meek and lowly Jesus. I thank you for the present you sent me, which I received as a token of love. The mission family are all well, and also the dear children. Many of them are serious, and we hope they love, and pray to God daily. O that I were more engaged for God, to promote his cause, among these dear children, and my people. I am going soon to visit my parents, which is an hundred miles from here, and expect to stay two months. I hope you will pray for me, that the Lord would bless my visit, and renew the hearts of my dear parents.

Your sincere friend and sister in Christ."

APPENDIX.

No. 4. Extracts from a letter written by the same person to her brother in the Foreign Mission School at Cornwall, dated,

"Cherokee nation, Aug. 1820.
* * * * "O dear brother, how much it would rejoice my heart to see you this evening, and converse with you face to face! But out good Lord has separated us, perhaps never to see each other again in this world. I often think of the morning you left Brainerd. It was a solemn hour, and I trust it was a sweet season to our souls. We wept, and prayed, and sung together before our dear Savior; and longed for that blessed day, when we should meet, to part no more. What is a short separation in this world? Nothing compared to an eternal separation! How thankful we ought to be then, my dear brother, that we have a hope to be saved through the blessed Lamb of God. Yes I trust when our bodies shall die, our souls shall be raised above the sky, where we shall dwell together, in singing the praises of Him who bought us with his precious blood. I hope we shall meet our parents, and brothers and sisters there. Since you left, the Lord has reached down his arm, to take sinners from darkness, into the marvellous light of the Gospel. Dear brother let us praise and rejoice continually in the Lord, for his goodness to our dear people, in giving them hearts to love and praise his holy name. Surely the Lord is with us here. We feel his presence. Our dear father and mother are inquiring what they shall do to be saved. Mother says she is grieved to think her children are going to leave her behind. But she says she will pray as long as she lives, and that the Savior will pardon her sins, that she may go with her children to heaven."

In another letter to the same person, of a more recent date, she says:

* * * * "Although we may be separated many hundreds of miles, the God of the Universe whom we serve, will often give us, the enjoyment of himself, which you know is of far greater value than all this world can afford.—— Last Sabbath was a

APPENDIX.

very solemn and interesting day to us. Rev. Mr. W. from the state of New York was here—a very pious and engaged Christian. We were much refreshed by his kind instructions. I think it was truly a pleasant day to my soul. The sacrament was administered, and we were permitted once more to sit at the table of the Lord, and commemorate his dying love. Mr. S. was baptized. Also an infant of Mrs. F. named SAMUEL WORCESTER. The congregation were attentive and some of them were affected to tears. I hope the time is not, far distant, when all the heathen shall be brought to the knowledge of the Redeemer. We have recently formed a Female Society[3] in this place. The members pay fifty cents a year. I trust you will pray that we may be blessed, and that we may be instrumental in the great work of building up the cause of the Redeemer. I can never be sufficiently thankful to God for sending us missionaries, to teach us the way we should go. We love them as our own brothers and sisters. That you may enjoy the light of our Savior's countenance, while in this short journey of life, and finally be received to mansions of eternal glory, is the prayer of your sister."

No. 5. Copy of a letter from a Choctaw youth, who left his native tribe in 1818, to obtain an education at the Foreign Mission School in Cornwall. It is addressed to the writer of the foregoing narrative, who conducted him from his tribe to the School, and taught him the English alphabet himself.

"Foreign Mission School, Cornwall, Conn.
Nov. 10, 1820.

"MY VERY DEAR SIR,

"It is now a great while since I saw you here, in this place, and therefore, I thought it would be convenient for me to write a few lines to you, and send it by Mr. George Sandwich, who is

---

[3] This Society is composed chiefly of Indian females who have been converted to Christianity.

APPENDIX.

now expecting to set out for the Sandwich Islands. May the Lord Jesus bless him, and grant him consolation and success on his way, and conduct him to his native country.

"Through the divine goodness, I yet enjoy a comfortable state of health. I have great reason to believe that the Lord Jesus Christ has recently renewed my wicked heart; and has showed me the path of everlasting righteousness above. I feel very thankful to God that he has brought me to this Christian land, where I can learn the good things of the religion of Christ,—and also I am very thankful to those good Christian people in this country, who are dear to us, and supplying all our wants. I do earnestly pray to God every day, that he may preserve me from the everlasting punishment. I hope I shall persevere in the path of duty which I have entered. I have lately felt a good deal about my dear, poor, fellow perishing countrymen, who are yet in the darkness and the shadow of death; and they know nothing about God, and the way of eternal life. But I am extremely rejoiced to learn that my brother D— is becoming a religious man. We had the pleasure of receiving a letter from him, on the first of Nov. He says he wishes to go to school, but has a great deal of business to do at home. He says, he is not too old to go to school, though he will be thirty years of age, next January. I should be very glad to have you to write a letter to him, as often as you think convenient, and give him good admonition, and encourage him to persevere in the path of righteousness.

"Now may the Lord Jesus Christ ever be with you and bless you, in all your undertakings, in doing a great deal of good in the world. I wish to be remembered with sincere affection to our dear, beloved, and venerable friend, Rev. Samuel Worcester, for whom I have a strong affection.

I am dear Sir, yours respectfully."

APPENDIX.

No. 6. The following is a copy of a letter written in 1818, by a Cherokee boy to his heathen parents. He had been a member of the Moravian school at Spring place about two years, and was at the time 14 years of age.

"Spring Place, April, 1818.

"DEAR FATHER AND MOTHER,

"I hope dear parents, that you will let me live with the Christians till I be a man, and once when I am come to our home, that I may be able to tell you about our Savior; for you never did hear about God how good he is to sinners, that if any body would pray to him, he would make him good and so live happy, and when they die he will take them up into heaven. And now let us love him, for he came down into this world to save us that we might be saved, if we believe him. I hope now you will pray to him, that he may make you good and happy and all of you there, and I shall pray for you too, and I hope mother, that you will pray to God to make you like your brother, he is a Christian and loves God. I hope I shall be once like him, be a Christian and love God. I will tell you about our Savior; he became a child and grew up and went about preaching to the people, but the wicked people went about to kill him. At last he knew that he should depart from this world to go to his father, and that he should suffer, and he went to a place, where was a garden, and he prayed three times and his sweat falling down to the ground, like as if it was great drops of blood, and an angel came and strengthened him, and he went to his disciples and they were all asleep, and as he yet spake, the people came and took him, and beat him and sent him to the Governor; he scourged him, and they put a crown of thorns upon his head, and they crucified him, and two malefactors with him, one on the left and the other on the right side, and they gave him vinegar to drink, and one good man took him down from the cross and buried him, and the third day he rose again from the dead. And he went up into heaven and now he lives forever, and sees all what we do, and if we do right and pray, he will bless us, and if

APPENDIX.

wrong, he will punish us. I hope you will think of this. But you cannot speak English, but you can pray to him in your own language. Pray to him who died on the cross for us. Give my love to all.

I remain your dutiful son."

No. 7. Copy of a letter from a Cherokee boy about thirteen years of age, who, when he came to Brainerd could speak no English. He is what is called, a full blooded Indian. The letter was written to the Author of this little book.

"Brainerd, Cherokee Nation, Feb. 1821.

"MY DEAR FRIEND,

* * * * * * "I have been here to school about two years and an half. A few years ago, I did not know that there was such learning as I have now got. But I often saw some of the people, those that had been to school awhile to some places, seeing that they had senses better than those that had not been to school. Now when this school was first commenced, I wanted to come very much indeed. But they would not let me come to school, because they thought that I was most too sickly to take hold of such work as that. But still I would not give up yet—a little while after that, I was just ready to come away without letting them know it. Miss H. happened to send for me to come to her house. O how glad I was to come to her house, hoping that she was going to take me here to school. When I got there her children were just ready to come to school. I rode on behind one of them. But yet not knowing that there was a Savior that came down from heaven to live, with his sorrowful heart, and acquainted with grief, to save his people from their sins. But now I know that he is holding his arms of mercy, calling on me, and all the people of the earth, both great and small, saying, "Come unto me all ye weary and heavy laden and I will give you rest."

* * * * * "Last June on Thursday morning I was out in the field; in about seven o'clock, I went up to the house, and I went into the porch to see Dr. Worcester, but when I got to the door, I

APPENDIX.

saw him drawing his last breath. Alas! what an awful thing it would be to see him drawing his last breath, if he had not been the friend of Jesus. But how great joy he had to rejoice for leaving this sinful world, to go to that happy world, where there is no sickness or death, into the bosom of his father Abraham, on the right hand of our Creator, to sing with the holy angels the song of Moses and the Lamb. I hope his children will try to follow their precious father. They laid the body in a house about two days and half, waiting for the Cherokees to come and see it. About in seven or eight o'clock, I saw some of my friends coming to see the body of our great friend, that who has done great good for the poor and benighted heathen nations, that they might be brought to a knowledge of Jesus Christ, and to hear what Mr. Hoyt would say to them. After the body was laid in the grave, we all went in the school house to hear Mr. Hoyt. After when he has finished talking to us, they all return to their home with most sorrowful heart for losing their great friend."

Let it be remembered that these youth, a few years ago, were wandering about in the forests of America, ignorant of christianity, and without any education such as civilized persons enjoy.

II.

EXTRACTS FROM A CORRESPONDENCE WITH A CONVERTED CHEROKEE CHIEF.[4]

The piece which follows, was drawn up in July, 1818, and contains a short account of the rise and progress of those improvements which had been made in the writer's tribe, to that time. It is entitled, "Sketch of the progress of Aboriginal Cherokees."

---

[4] This chief learned to read and write the English language when young.

APPENDIX.

"The great and good Washington said to the Cherokees, 'As you now find the game growing scarce, and when you cannot meet a deer to kill, you will remain hungry and naked, and without other implements than the hoe to till the ground, you will continue to raise scanty crops of corn; hence you are exposed to suffer from hunger and cold, and as the game are lessening in numbers, more and more, these sufferings will increase, and how are you to provide against them? and said, listen to my words, some of you already experience the advantage of keeping cattle and hogs; let all keep them, and increase their numbers.'

"Such was the language held out to the Cherokees, which objects had directed the steps of our former Agent, Silas Dinsmore, who, seating himself in the centre of the nation, and held out to the Cherokee warriors, the plough, the axe and the mattock, with the pledge of the olive branch, over the lands, encouraging them to cultivate, and raise corn, cotton and stock on the land, and stimulating the females, in the language of a brother, with wheels, cards, and the loom, to spin and weave their own clothing. Yet such sudden changes of habits and pursuits, were productive of jealousies, which was indeed natural, but these jealousies subsided with the advantages to the individuals, who had made the first trial of the advices given them.

"Such were the inducement, which was held out to the Cherokees, that made it necessary to mature its advantages, before it could be perceptible, and in the lapse of four or five years they began to use some more industry in families of raising cotton, for there were only two or three wheels, and cards, and no loom in the nation, when these encouragements were brought forward in our council; and to change to the habits and pursuits which had been recommended to them, they began to move to separate farms from the towns; still the towns claimed jurisdiction over those persons who had so separated themselves from the community to which they had belonged to.

APPENDIX.

"Seventeen years has passed, since the Cherokees have begun to separate themselves into separate families, over the country which pertain to them, between the waters Tennessee and Chattahouchie rivers, and in some instances have gone over those rivers.

"Considerable advances have been made by the Cherokees, since they have settled on separate farms, in agriculture, and their own clothing, and these advances has been more or less beneficial, in the circumscribing of our limits, by repeated sales of our lands, and the game less sought after now than a few years back, as they begin to find that the products of the earth and labor, are the sure pledges of independence.

"Numbers of private schools are kept in different parts of the nation, and other charitable schools are established to educate the Cherokee youth, which will promote the civilization and christianization in a high degree."

In another communication he says,

"Although separated by far distant and distinct family of the human race, yet but one flesh. It will be the greatest comforts, and joy of my life, to hear of your welfare, in the service of the all atoning Master, who will prosper thy labors among the Red men of America, that they may come to the tree of life, and drink the healing stream when thirsty, and that they may sing the song of redeeming love, of God their Savior.

III.

EXTRACTS FROM A CORRESPONDENCE WITH A CHOCTAW CHIEF.

The letters, from which the following extracts are made, were written at different times; and relate chiefly, to the institution of schools and other means of instruction among the Choctaws.

APPENDIX.

* * * * * * * * * * * * *

"I know, and all I can say for my nation, they are people much in need for help, and instruction. And we look up to the Government of the United States for instruction—and which I do know, the establishment of this school,[5] will be the means of the greatest work ever been done for this nation."

"I have just returned from the Choctaw treaty, and I inform you that the Choctaws did not sell or exchange their lands, with the United States. The Choctaws said, that it is but two years ago when nation sold a large track of country to the United States, and therefore they said that they had no more lands to sell—which they cannot think to sell the land which we are living on it, and raising our children on it."

* * * * * * * * * * * * *

"I am anxious, and waiting to see the great day to appear, before we poor distress't Red peoples—hoping that the day of light will come before we Choctaws. We are ignorance, we are in the darke, and therefore we must humbly ask for help from our Christian brethren, as a poor helpless children look up to their father crying to have pity on them.

"I am much in hope McK. and I.,[6] are sensible the advantages of good education, and that they will exert their utmost, all their abilities to improve their time in the very best manner."

* * * * * * * * * * * * *

"Dear friend, you will understand, that you good people of the north, have led us to the knowledge of great good, of white path. And we Red people have listen to your good counsel, and we Choctaws have discovered the day light approaching, for us good by taking your counsel. Lead us in this white path that we may find the great joy and happiness as you do."

"There is a great many indeed in the nation, whom it might be supposed they would care nothing about learning, and that they should be considered, that they are so ignorant that they never would be brought about to believe that learning, was good

---

[5] The school at Elliot.
[6] Brothers of the chief, at the Cornwall school.

APPENDIX.

things; but to the contrary. I am glad to say to you, this day, on this paper that Choctaws are in throughout the whole nation, are anxious for schools. Now I wish to tell you how my nation are since they became acquainted with our beloved Missionaries, and never before seen a such a school, and not more, or hardly year since, our Red children were sent to this school at Elliot, and now they can read and write some. Choctaw nation are both hands are open for more missionaries, more schools."

"You will excuse my bad writing as I did inform you, that I had only but six months schooling."

THE END.

Index

ALEXANDER 10
ALMIGHTY GOD 96,99
ARCH, John 30,37,55
BACON 86
BASCOM
   Mr 59,76
   Rev Reynolds......................59,75
BEAR-MEAT 48
BETSEY....................................... 10
BLACKBURN, Rev Gideon 11
BOUDINOT, Mr 70
BRAINERD, David................13,131
BROTHER DAVID.............60,66,70
BROTHER JOHN...................56,84
BROTHER POTTER 76
BROTHER W.............................. 68
BROTHER WALTER................ 68
BROWN...................................... 10
   Catharine.......9,10,21,23,25,28,29,
   32,34,35,42,43,44,62,63,64,65,70,
   71,75,76,85,95,96,100,101,147
   Col Dick 10
   David...............................9,10,40
   John..9,10
   Mr 10,27,30,31,36,37,40,48,76
   Mr & Mrs................................ 10
   Mr John 10,48
   Mrs... 10
   Polly....................................... 10
   Sarah 10
   Susan 10
   Susannah 10
BUTLER, Dr............................... 60
BUTRICK
   Mr 38,40,48,55
   Rev Daniel S 37
   Rev Mr 36
CALHOUN, John C 122
CAMPBELL
   Dr 58,69,72,74,75,77,78,80,
   82,83,92,93
   Dr Alexander A 58
   Mrs 72,74
CARTER
   Lydia 25,119,124,127,128,129,
   131,138,140,142,143,144,146,147,
   148,149,153,154
   Mrs 122

   Mrs Lydia 119
CATHARINE...... 12,13,14,16,17,18,
19,20,21,22,24,26,30,31,36,38,39,40,41,
45,46,47,48,49,50,57,59,66,67,72,73,
77,78,79,80,81,82,83,87,88,91,92,93,97,
99,125,145
CHAMBERLAIN
   Brother..................................... 28
   Catharine 140,154
   Mr ...128,129,138,139,140,141,142
   Mr & Mrs 28,125,138
   Mrs 22,154
   Rev Mr................................... 154
   Rev William 17,125
   Sister.......................................28
CHRIST.......... 18,22,24,29,31,32,33,
41,42,47,49,56,57,62,66,77,78,89,90,
94,95,136,154,156,159
CLARK
   Gov... 125
   Governor............. 122,126,127,142
   William............................ 122,126
CORNELIUS
   Mr.....................................34,140
   Rev Elias 17,25
DAVID............ 17,18,30,36,38,43,46,
64,72,74,76,77,80
DINSMORE, Silas 163
DR C 80
DWIGHT, President 148
EDMUND 10
EVARTS
   Jeremiah 20,120
   Mr 21,120,122,126
FOLSOM, Israel 69
G
   Mr...53
   Sister..53
GALUNLAHRIAHI......................88
GAMBOLD, Mr & Mrs.................23
GILBRETH, Mrs 10,45
GOD..12,15,16,17,18,19,21,24,27,28,
29,30,31,32,33,34,35,36,41,42,43,44,46,
49,51,52,53,54,55,56,57,58,60,63,64,
65,67,68,70,74,75,76,77,78,80,81,82,87,
88,89,90,91,92,93,95,97,99,100,101,
123,125,127,129,135,136,139,142,146,
149,150,151,156,157,158,159,160,164

Index

HALL
   Mr 37
   Mr & Mrs 32,35,40,62,65
   Mr Moody 13,34
   Mrs Isabella 42
HICKS
   Brother 142
   Mr 142
HOYT
   Father 28
   Milo 145
   Mr 21,25,26,51,52,127,128, 129,147,162
   Rev Ard 21,123
JACKSON, General 12
JACOB 39
JEHOVAH 88
JESUS 35,44,51,56,69,70,84,93, 135,152,156,162
JESUS CHRIST .. 16,23,35,36,43,52, 55,68,125,135,162
JOHN 45,52,54,57,63,68
JOSEPH 39
KINGSBURY
   Brother & Sister 34
   Mr 14,18,21,28,113,117, 119,123,131,136
   Rev Cyrus 13,117
   Rev Mr 96
LAMB OF GOD 61
LEECH
   Mr 90
   Mr William 78
LITTLE JOHN 146,147,149
LOCKE 86
LOONEY, Mrs 10
LORD 15,18,27,32,35,42,43,46, 50,52,53,55,61,77,151
LORD JESUS ... 47,78,94,96,156,159
LORD JESUS CHRIST 17,36,88, 159
LOVELY, Mrs 150
LOWRY, Lydia 27
LYDIA 129,139,145,155
MCKEE 69
MCKENNEY, Thomas L 122
MEIGS
   Col 25,123,127,128

   Colonel 142,143
MILLER, Governor 143,147,148,149
MILO 28,29,145
MISS H 161
MOSES 162
MOST HIGH 19
MR J R 54
MR S 65,158
MRS C 78
MRS F 65,158
MRS L 78
MRS P 69,75,96
NEWTON 86
P, Mr & Mrs 52
POLLY 10
POTTER
   Mr 48,52,53,59,69,75,77
   Mr & Mrs 47,50,56
   Mrs 45,48,72,76,79,80,81, 90,92,93,95
   Rev Mr 58
   Rev William 45
REV MR W 65,158
ROGERS
   Mr 144
   Mr John 143
ROSS
   John Osage 25,129,143,144,149
   Mr 25,129
   Mr John 25,128
SANDWICH, Mr George 158
SARAH 9,10
SAVIOR 27
SAVIOUR 51
SISTER A 148
SISTER ANNA 61
SISTER FLORA 29
SISTER POTTER 73
ST PAUL 86
SUSAN 10,70,82
SUSANNAH 52,54,68
TA-LON-TIS-KEE, General 155
TSA-LUH 9
WALTER 10
WAU-SAU-SEY 48
WEBBER, Col 10
WILLIAMS
   Brother 33

Index

Mr 28
Mr & Mrs 33
Mr Loring S 13
Mrs 27,34,119
Sister 33
WILSON
   Alice.. 27
   Mr 27
   Peggy 27
WORCESTER............................137
   Dr............................20,52,131,161
   Rev Dr....................................134
   Rev Samuel............................159
   Samuel 65,158
WOTTEE 10
YAU-NU-GUNG-YAH-SKI 9

Other Books and Series by Jeff Bowen

- *Census of the Osage Indians of Osage Agency, Oklahoma, 1906-1929*
  - *1906-1911 Volume I*
  - *1912-1916 Volume II*   **Coming Soon!**

(More volumes to come)

➢ Softback ISBN: 978-1-64968-176-8

Other Books and Series by Jeff Bowen

COMPLIMENT THE OSAGE SERIES WITH A UNIQUE GENEALOGICAL AND HISTORY BOOK OF THE OSAGE NATION

History of the Osage Nation

Its People, Resources, and Prospects
The Last Reservation to Open in the New State
by Philip Dickerson, M.A.

Transcribed by
Jeff Bowen

- Hardback ISBN: 978-1-64968-177-5
- Softback ISBN: 978-1-64968-178-2

Other Books and Series by Jeff Bowen

- *Cherokee Granted Enrollment Cards & Dawes Packets 1900 – 1907 Volumes I, II, III & IV*

    (More volumes to come)

COMPLIMENT ALL CHEROKEE SERIES WITH THE GREATEST CHEROKEE HISTORY AND GENEALOGICAL BOOK PUBLISHED!

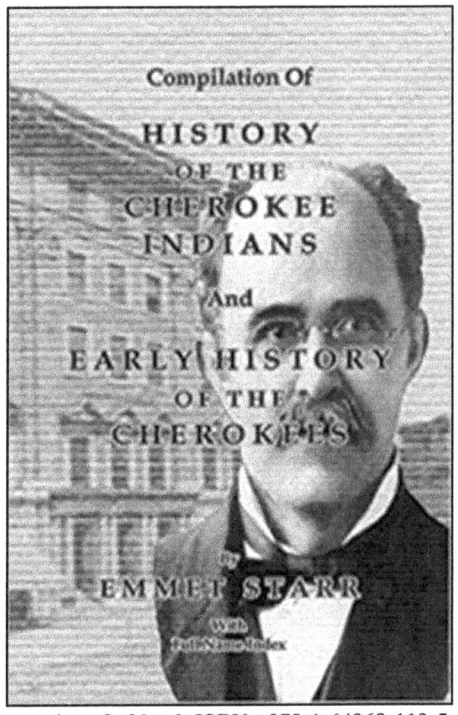

➤ Softback ISBN: 978-1-64968-119-5
➤ Hardback ISBN: 978-1-64968-127-0

Other Books and Series by Jeff Bowen

Other Cherokee Publications You May Not Know About

- *Compilation of History of the Cherokee Indians and Early History of the Cherokees* by Emmet Starr *with Combined Full Name Index* (Hardback & Softback)

- *Eastern Cherokee by Blood, 1906-1910, Volumes I* thru *XIII*

- *Eastern Cherokee Census Cherokee, North Carolina 1930-1939 Census 1930-1931 with Births And Deaths 1924-1931 Taken By Agent L. W. Page Volume I*
- *Eastern Cherokee Census Cherokee, North Carolina 1930-1939 Census 1932-1933 with Births And Deaths 1930-1932 Taken By Agent R. L. Spalsbury Volume II*
- *Eastern Cherokee Census Cherokee, North Carolina 1930-1939 Census 1934-1937 with Births and Deaths 1925-1938 and Marriages 1936 & 1938 Taken by Agents R. L. Spalsbury And Harold W. Foght Volume III*

- *Starr Roll 1894 (Cherokee Payment Rolls) Districts: Canadian, Cooweescoowee, and Delaware Volume One*
- *Starr Roll 1894 (Cherokee Payment Rolls) Districts: Flint, Going Snake, and Illinois Volume Two*
- *Starr Roll 1894 (Cherokee Payment Rolls) Districts: Saline, Sequoyah, and Tahlequah; Including Orphan Roll Volume Three*

- *Cherokee Descendants East An Index to the Guion Miller Applications Volume I*
- *Cherokee Descendants West An Index to the Guion Miller Applications Volume II (A-M)*
- *Cherokee Descendants West An Index to the Guion Miller Applications Volume III (N-Z)*

- *Cherokee Intruder Cases Dockets of Hearings 1901-1909 Volumes I & II*

Other Books and Series by Jeff Bowen

- *Eastern Cherokee Census, Cherokee, North Carolina, 1915-1922, Taken by Agent James E. Henderson*
    - *Volume I (1915-1916)*
    - *Volume II (1917-1918)*
    - *Volume III (1919-1920)*
    - *Volume IV (1921-1922)*

- *Eastern Cherokee Census, Cherokee, North Carolina, 1923-1929, Taken by Agent James E. Henderson*
    - *Volume I (1923-1924)*
    - *Volume II (1925-1926)*
    - *Volume III (1927-1929)*

- *Texas Cherokees 1820-1839 A Document For Litigation 1921*

- *North Carolina Eastern Cherokee Indian Census 1898-1899, 1904, 1906, 1909-1912, 1914 Revised and Expanded Edition*

- *Cherokee Citizenship Commission Dockets 1880-1884 and 1887-1889 Volumes I thru V*

- *Cherokee Intermarried White 1906 Volume I thru X*

- *Cherokee Granted Enrollment Cards & Dawes Packets 1900 - 1907 Volumes I, II & III*

Visit our website at *www.nativestudy.com* to learn more about these other books and series by Jeff Bowen